The
IDENTITY
Journey

KENDALL LAUGHLIN, JR.

≈ i ≈

AN INTRODUCTION
TO THE IDENTITY JOURNEY

I awoke early the morning of my thirty-first birthday. After setting up my coffee and putting on some music I sat down for my rhythm of spending time with God.

This was an unusual morning for me because I had woken up early without incident. With small children in the home and also being pretty much the opposite of a "morning person," spending time with God in the mornings can sometimes be a fight. I sat down and took a sip of my coffee as I extended my heart out to the Lord. It was then that I heard what some describe as God's "still small voice."

> *"I want to give you a present for your birthday today."*

It began just like a whisper but the clarity of the words grew in my spirit. I knew that God was wanting to reveal something to me. Also, I've been walking with God long enough now to know that the "present" described was probably *not* going to be a Ferrari.

I leaned in…

> *"I want to give you a present today… there are 31 Promises for your life, and they are all in the book of Ephesians."*

I eagerly opened my Bible app and began to read through the book of Ephesians, line-by-line. This began my journey; my upgrade into new a confidence in my identity in Christ. My new identity was found in some ancient promises… hidden in the Scriptures.

I want to invite you upon this journey as well.
May the next 31 days become a remarkable discovery of your identity.

How I First Learned the Power of Identity

For most of us, disorientation leads to discovery. My story is no exception. I initially learned the power of the believer's identity in Christ during a disorienting and confusing season as a freshman in college.

My Disorientation

Being raised in the Christian tradition, I knew the teachings of the Bible when I attended university in 2001, but was hungry for more. I had recently had a spiritual awakening, a turning point, as a senior in high school. I was eager to attend a Christian college and to find God's will for my life.

It's easy to think that if we make a big choice to obey God (for me, attending a Christian college was such a choice, and a big diversion from my life plan), then everything will immediately start going our way. Although I do believe that God loves to bless and prosper His people, I have also found that after big steps towards Jesus, a testing period comes into one's life. Sometimes these tests come in the form of spiritual warfare. Other times tests come as God allows us to see the limits of our human strength. For me, I experienced both. I had begun my disorientation away from "my plan" to "God's plan."

During that year, I came to the end of myself. I remember one late night, walking, praying, and hoping to hear the voice of God. I began to have the revelation that God had allowed some discipline and failure in my life to give me the opportunity to rely on Him.

A random Scripture came to my mind, *Isaiah 7:9*. I turned to my Bible and I was amazed to read Isaiah 7:9 for what was probably the first time:

> *"If you do not stand firm in faith, you shall not stand at all."*

That was a very needed word.

Spiritual warfare, anxiety, and relationship drama became themes in my life over the next few months. It was the Fall of 2001 and the world was in turmoil due to 9/11. It was a dark, emotional time in our nation.

Personally, I was also in a tailspin. I had always been a bright student, but those first few months at university I began to experience the shame and frustration of academic failure. I had a harder time finding my footing socially at a Christian college than I expected. Eventually I wondered if I had made the wrong decision about school.

A Discovery

I realized eventually that regardless of what university I attended, my issues were of the heart. Circumstances wouldn't change my inner world. I needed to learn how to "stand in faith". I began to go deeper into relationship with God, walking with faith-filled friends, and attending a Spirit-empowered church. I finally got serious about prayer, and even fasted for the first time. But there was still something that was not "clicking."

It was during this time in my life that I began to be discipled. "Discipleship," or mentoring, is simply regularly meeting with a more mature believer for the purposes of growing in God. During this time of discipleship, Robert (my mentor) gave me a book called "Victory Over the Darkness" by Neil Anderson. The book contained powerful truths and secrets regarding the believer's identity in Christ.

Neil Anderson's powerful teaching, about us being secure, significant, and accepted in Christ, worked its way into my spiritual DNA. At the end of the book was a sheet titled "Who I am in Christ." Robert told me about the power of speaking God's word out loud and, being desperate, I took his advice literally. I remember actually locking myself in the closet of my freshman dorm room in order to vocalize those Scriptures without hindrance. This powerful discovery began a powerful time of transformation in my life. I had embarked upon an identity journey.

Truth Revisited

Because this truth of identity had become so foundational in my life in college , it was a surprise to me when, in my thirties, God seemed to be re-emphasizing this concept of identity.

I had taught about identity in ministry schools and even preached on the subject in large settings. But I could sense that God was reviewing this truth with me. He wanted to take me further and deeper.

Something happened to me at 31 years of age when I began to declare and meditate on these these re-discovered promises. I crossed a threshold. I began to finally believe that "He who began a good work in me would bring it to completion (Phillipians 1:6)." I began to place my confidence in *God's supernatural power* rather than in my own *super-spirituality*.

When we become established in our identity in Christ we begin to realize that our faith journey is utterly dependent on Jesus's finished work.

Our Identity is a Supernatural Work of God

Christianity by nature is supernatural, and our supernatural journey starts with understanding our identity in Christ.

The "Apostle's Creed," which is one of the most commonly accepted belief statements by Christians throughout the globe, points to the supernatural reality that undergirds our faith in Jesus. Read it below:

> *"I believe in God, the Father almighty, creator of heaven and earth. I believe in Jesus Christ, God's only Son, our Lord, who was conceived by the Holy Spirit, born of the Virgin Mary, suffered under Pontius Pilate, was crucified, died, and was buried; he descended to the dead. On the third day he rose again; he ascended into heaven, he is seated at the right hand of the Father, and he will come to judge the living and the dead. I believe in the Holy Spirit, the holy catholic Church, the communion of saints, the forgiveness of sins, the resurrection of the body, and the life everlasting. Amen."*
> **The Apostle's Creed**

To summarize the Apostle's Creed… *"God created heaven and earth. He sent His Son, Our Lord to that earth in the form of a miraculous conception. Jesus came to the earth, lived a perfect life, performed many miracles, and then died to forgive the sins of all mankind. After raising Himself from the death, Christ ascended to Heaven to rule all galaxies and governments! "*

Just as we see God's supernatural power at work through the Gospel message we received and believe, we also can trust that God's supernatural power is at work in our identity. Your identity in Christ is not something that can be stolen or taken away. It has been purchased by the blood of Jesus, supernaturally.

The Benefits of Understanding Identity

A revelation of identity will give you peace, security, and well-being because your emotional and spiritual state will no longer be based on your own religious duty. The truth that we are accepted by God allows us to breathe deep and enjoy life.

> "Religion: 'My identity is built on being a good person.'
> Gospel: 'My identity is not built on... my performance but on Christ's.
> **Tim Keller**

Consciousness of your position and identity in Christ will open doors for God's miraculous power to flow through your life. For the believer to truly experience the miraculous, he or she must eventually reach a point where they have a greater faith in God's goodness than spiritual performance, special gifts, financial resources, or earthly wisdom. Nothing supernatural can be accomplished by our own strength.

No matter what lies the Devil has told you or what hardships you have been through, Jesus has given you an identity card that gives you access to the supernatural life. As you read these 31 promises over the next few days my desire is for you to know that these promises are for you, today.

As we begin our 31 Day Identity Journey, read Ephesians Chapters 1 and 2 for yourself. Allow the truth of who God says you are to prepare your heart for the journey ahead.

Ephesians 1 & 2, English Standard Version

Paul, an apostle of Christ Jesus by the will of God, To the saints who are in Ephesus, and are faithful in Christ Jesus:

Grace to you and peace from God our Father and the Lord Jesus Christ.

Blessed be the God and Father of our Lord Jesus Christ, who has blessed us in Christ with every spiritual blessing in the heavenly places, even as he chose us in him before the foundation of the world, that we should be holy and blameless before him. In love he predestined us for adoption to himself as sons through Jesus Christ, according to the purpose of his will, to the praise of his glorious grace, with which he has blessed us in the Beloved. In him we have redemption through his blood, the forgiveness of our trespasses, according to the riches of his grace, which he lavished upon us, in all wisdom and insight making known to us the mystery of his will, according to his purpose, which he set forth in Christ as a plan for the fullness of time, to unite all things in him, things in heaven and things on earth.

In him we have obtained an inheritance, having been predestined according to the purpose of him who works all things according to the counsel of his will, so that we who were the first to hope in Christ might be to the praise of his glory. In him you also, when you heard the word of truth, the gospel of your salvation, and believed in him, were sealed with the promised Holy Spirit, who is the guarantee of our inheritance until we acquire possession of it, to the praise of his glory.

For this reason, because I have heard of your faith in the Lord Jesus and your love toward all the saints, I do not cease to give thanks for you, remembering you in my prayers, that the God of our Lord Jesus Christ, the Father of glory, may give you the Spirit of wisdom and of revelation in the knowledge of him, having the eyes of your hearts enlightened, that you may know what is the hope to which he has called you, what are the riches of his glorious inheritance in the saints, and what is the immeasurable greatness of his power toward us who believe, according to the working of his great might that he worked in Christ when he raised him from the dead and seated him at his right hand in the heavenly places, far above all rule and authority and power and dominion, and above every name that is named, not only in this age but also in the one to come. And he put all things under his feet and gave him as head over all things to the church, which is his body, the fullness of him who fills all in all.

And you were dead in the trespasses and sins in which you once walked, following the course of this world, following the prince of the power of the air, the spirit that is now at work in the sons of disobedience— among whom we all once lived in the passions of our flesh, carrying out the desires of the body and the mind, and were by nature children of wrath, like the rest of mankind. But God, being rich in mercy, because of the great love with which he loved us, even when we were dead in our trespasses, made us alive together with Christ—by grace you have been saved—and raised us up with him and seated us with him in the heavenly places in Christ Jesus, so that in the coming ages he might show the immeasurable riches of his grace in kindness toward us in Christ Jesus. For by grace you have been saved through faith. And this is not your own doing; it is the gift of God, not a result of works, so that no one may boast. For we are his workmanship, created in Christ Jesus for good works, which God prepared beforehand, that we should walk in them.

≈ ii ≈

THE 31 DAY JOURNEY

During the next 31 days we will review 31 promises of your identity in Christ found in the book of Ephesians. As you begin to meditate upon and declare God's word over your life, I am believing you will experience lasting transformation.

Practical Instructions:

1. For 31 days read the devotional for that day. Every devotion will be based upon a selection from Ephesians 1-2:10.

    Don't worry about missing a day. Start right back if you fall behind.

2. After reading each day's passage turn to the page titled, "The Declarations List" (next page).

3. **Say the declarations, aloud, daily** (It's important to vocalize God's Word aloud - the Bible speaks many times about the power of the tongue).

    This is the most important step of the devotional for each day.

4. For deeper study, read Ephesians 1 and 2 yourself and highlight any specific promises God reveals to you above and beyond these.

5. Continue to refer back to this list as a guide during seasons in life when you need to be more firmly established in your identity in Christ.

The Declarations List

I am a saint.

I have grace and peace.

I am already blessed with every spiritual blessing.

I am chosen.

I am holy and blameless before God.

I am adopted into God's family.

I am beloved by God and in the beloved of God.

I am redeemed and forgiven through His blood.

I have lavishly received grace.

I have a purpose.

I know the mystery of God's will.

I have an inheritance.

I am the praise of Christ's glory.

I am sealed with the Holy Spirit.

I have a heavenly father.

I have wisdom.

I have revelation.

I have eyes that see what God is doing.

I have the hope of His calling.

I have glorious riches.

I have God's power working towards me.

I have Christ as my Head.

I am in Christ's body.

I have received Christ's fullness.

I am loved with a great love.

I am spiritually alive.

I am seated in heavenly places.

I have received a free gift from God.

I have more grace and kindness than can be measured.

I am God's workmanship.

I am created to do good works.

WE ARE SAINTS

Mother Theresa was known worldwide for her personal sacrifice, charity to the poor, and gentleness of spirit. People were known to travel from far and wide to experience her ministry, the Missionaries of Charity in Calcutta, India. Theresa of Calcutta met with many world leaders, received the Nobel Peace Prize, and received the prestigious Presidential Medal of Freedom from President Ronald Reagan.

Theresa died on September 5, 1997, 47 years after founding the Missionaries of Charity. Because of Theresa's great impact and devout life on earth it was only natural for those who respect the Catholic tradition to ask the question, "Will Mother Theresa become a saint?" In the Roman Catholic tradition, those who are recognized by the church for their unusual virtue are awarded the title of "Saint" after death. Eventually, Theresa's sainthood was recognized by the Catholic church in 2016 through a process called canonization.

The truth is, even prior to her canonization on September 4, 2016, when Pope Francis recognized Theresa as a saint, she already was one! **All believers are saints in Jesus Christ.**

Are you aware that the Bible calls all believers "saints?" The New Testament refers to God's people as saints 61 times! Paul refers to followers of Jesus as saints in almost every one of his Biblical letters. Ephesians 1:1 begins sharing that the book of Ephesians was written to saints.

> *"The <u>saints</u> who are in Ephesus, and are faithful in Christ Jesus;"*
> **Ephesians 1:1**

The word saint is translated from the greek *hagios* literally meaning "holy ones" or those who are "set apart."

Unfortunately, a drawback of the veneration of historical Christians as special saints is that many believers never fully understand their own identity as saints in God's Kingdom. Sainthood seems unattainable. It is more common in the church today to hear Christians share that they are *sinners saved by grace*. But this is not the language the Bible uses. Even books of the Bible written to Christians dealing with sinful behavior, like 1 Corinthians, refer to believers as *"saints"* (1 Corinthians 1:2).

The foundation of our identity in Christ is an understanding of the work that Jesus has already done in us. When a man or woman receives the forgiveness of Jesus Christ, he or she is permanently changed. Their identity, their very being, and their spirit becomes totally new. They become a "new creation" (2 Cor 5:17). Although after meeting Jesus we may struggle with sin, our status is no longer as a sinner but as a saint. We have a victorious identity.

The book of Ephesians beautifully contrasts the new creation we are in Christ as saints with our former life of sin. Notice how Paul uses the *past tense* (examples underlined) in describing our sinful behavior and patterns prior to meeting Christ.

> *"And you were dead in the trespasses and sins in which you once walked, following the course of this world, following the prince of the power of the air, the spirit that is now at work in the sons of disobedience— among whom we all once lived in the passions of our flesh, carrying out the desires of the body and the mind, and were by nature children of wrath, like the rest of mankind. But God, being rich in mercy, because of the great love with which he loved us, even when we were dead in our trespasses, made us alive together with Christ—by grace you have been saved— and raised us up with him and seated us with him in the heavenly places in Christ Jesus, so that in the coming ages he might show the immeasurable riches of his grace in kindness toward us in Christ Jesus. For by grace you have been saved through faith. And this is not your own doing; it is the gift of God, not a result of works, so that no one may boast."*
> **Ephesians 2:1-9**

Understanding the righteousness you now have in Christ is the foundation of this journey of identity. Although we will struggle with sin, we can have victory in our life over sinful behavior - because it's not who we are.

Our "sainthood' in Christ empowers us in our struggle for freedom and also allows us to be fully accepted by God. We have become righteous in God's eyes.

> *"For our sake he made him to be sin who knew no sin, so that in him we might become the righteousness of God."*
> **2 Corinthians 5:21**

Your beliefs empower your behaviors. If you believe you are a sinner, you will continue to be lost in sin. But if you believe God's work has formed you to be righteous... the possibilities are endless.

Begin to think of yourself as a saint who has been saved from being a sinner. You are a new creation in Christ. This is the foundation of the transformational journey in understanding our identity in Christ.

ALL BELIEVERS ARE SAINTS IN JESUS CHRIST.

≍ 2 ≍

WE HAVE GRACE AND PEACE

Social scientists comment that the tone of any interaction is set in the first five minutes. For me, I remember my parents reminding me as I went off to school, "You only have one chance to make a first impression."

If it's true that first impressions are important (and that the tone for any interaction is set in the first few minutes), then how we greet one another becomes a priority in our conversations. A greeting from another can make us feel like an insider or an outsider, accepted or rejected, a valued customer or an inconvenience. We've all experienced both.

Being a letter to the early church, the book of Ephesians begins with a greeting. Paul's greeting to the Ephesians, and to us today as readers, is significant. He speaks over the church a blessing of "grace and peace."

> *"Grace to you and peace from God our Father and the Lord Jesus Christ."*
> **Ephesians 1:2**

The Greek word *charis,* meaning grace, was a common greeting in the Ancient world. Much like a warm greeting, grace is something that is given, not earned. The greeting of another with "grace" is a way to show unbiased acceptance and favor at the beginning of a conversation. Grace puts us at ease. Grace empowers us to be transformed.

Grace is ours in Jesus Christ.

The word peace as a greeting has its origins in the famous Hebrew greeting *shalom*.

Strong's Bible dictionary points to the multiple meanings of the Hebrew word *shalom*: "ease, favor, friendship, health, peace, perfect peace, prosperity, safety, welfare, and wholeness". Greeting one another with *shalom*, or "peace," is a statement of prophetic blessing.

Grace and peace are ours because they are "from God our Father and the Lord Jesus Christ." We don't earn grace and peace. They are given to us freely because of the nature of our Heavenly Father.

It's interesting that Paul uses the traditional greetings of two different, and at the time of writing, *opposing* ethnicities. This inclusion of a Greek and a Hebrew greeting points to the acceptance by Jesus of all peoples. Regardless of your ethnicity or religious background, Jesus accepts you.

You have grace and peace and we as believers can experience grace and peace together because of the work of Jesus Christ.

IT'S ALREADY

BEEN PAID FOR.

WE ARE ALREADY BLESSED WITH EVERY SPIRITUAL BLESSING

"It's already been paid for."

Have you ever heard these five words at a surprising time?

For our tenth wedding anniversary my wife and I were able to take a trip to New York City. It was our first time on vacation without our children after several years of ministry. During our trip I was able to get us a dinner appointment with an old friend who is a bit of New York restaurant aficionado. New York City is home to many world renowned restaurants, so I knew it would be a fun night together.

As my friend and I were discussing dinner, he sent us some options of places to meet. I began to look at the menus online and was a little surprised. Just one of these meals would burst our food budget for the entire weekend!

My friend ended up talking us into joining him. We met him at a restaurant that had just been written up in the New York Times for its avant garde approach to cooking. It was truly the meal of a lifetime. The food, the service, and the experience were flawless. I couldn't even describe some of the dishes in writing if I tried, but if you've never had a bacon-infused marshmallow… let me tell you, you are missing out!

When the check came, my friend looked at us and said, "It's already been paid for." My wife and I were blessed beyond belief (and a little relieved!) by my friend's generosity. It's a special memory.

As we stepped out of the restaurant to head to the theatre I looked above the door. Written just above the threshold of the building, in about 20 foot letters, was the word GRACE. New Yorkers will know that this refers to the WR Grace building near Bryant Park. Having enjoyed such an exquisite meal at the expense of a friend, the word definitely took on new meaning that night.

Grace is a powerful word. Preachers sometimes quote that "GRACE" is an acronym for...

God's   *Riches*   *At*   *Christ's*   *Expense*

It's amazing to think that in the Kingdom of God, "it's already been paid for." Because of grace, the Bible says, "we've been blessed with every spiritual blessing" in the heavenly realms. Our life is no longer about earning our own way, getting what we're owed, or fighting for acceptance and provision.

Paul writes,

> *"Blessed be the God and Father of our Lord Jesus Christ, who has <u>blessed us with every spiritual blessing</u> in the heavenly places..."*
> **Ephesians 1:3**

Notice that Paul writes in the past-tense. God "*has* blessed." Jesus has already done it all for us. Our life is now simply a response of worship to the blessing of our Heavenly Father.

Getting practical, how are we to respond to God when we have needs, knowing that we have been blessed by Him, through Jesus?

Ephesians 1:3 gives us the key of how to respond when we have practical needs. The verse starts with the phrase "Blessed be the God and Father..." This is a phase of worship. In some translations, the word is "praise. When we choose praise and thanksgiving, God breaks in on our behalf. Multiplication comes when we thank the Father for what He has already provided.

God has done more for us than we could ever imagine.

"It's already been paid for."

⸝ **4** ⸝

WE ARE CHOSEN

Our church family hosts a ministry school that ends each class ministry and prayer. At the end of ones evening's session, I felt that the Lord wanted to give a student a simple word, "You are chosen."

At the end of the night the student approached me and shared that earlier in the day she had been spending some extra time with the Lord through journaling and prayer. She had literally written out in her journal, "God, show me today that I am chosen."

We all have a deep desire to be chosen. A common definition of chosen might be "to be wanted, to be accepted, and to be recognized as having a distinct purpose." The Merriam Webster dictionary defines one who is chosen as a "object of divine choice or favor."

Many of us have felt the pain of being "un-chosen." Everyone at times has been overlooked for the team, ignored by their superior for a big promotion, or simply just felt left out. The brokenness of our social world, affected by the weight of sin, causes all of us to feel the insecurity of rejection.

> *"he chose us in him before the creation of the world..."*
> **Ephesians 1:4**

The amazing thing about Jesus's death on the cross was that the Father gave Jesus a choice. In the darkness of Gethsemane, Jesus stared death in the face and prayed "Father, if you are willing, take this cup from me; yet not my will, but yours be done" (Luke 22:42). It's fascinating to consider that Jesus the Savior submitted His will to God, the Father. He did this as our example and to demonstrate the supreme act of love committed by *choosing* us.

When Jesus died on the cross, He chose you and me. He chose to suffer for your specific sins, shortcomings, and failures. And through His resurrection He chose to make you a new person with purpose.

Your chosen-ness by God is not just demonstrated your salvation. It is also demonstrated by your unique gifts, purpose and calling. God is writing a unique story through your life.

The Psalmist writes:

> *"Your eyes saw my unformed body; all the days ordained for me were written in your book before one of them came to be."*
> **Psalm 139:16**

Have you every wondered what is written in the book of your life? You may have wondered what kind of story your life will be. Or, like Frodo Baggins, what kind of "tale you've fallen into." Whatever your story is, you have been chosen for something special.

The ancient Hebrews believed each person's uniqueness was divinely appointed. Some Rabbis even taught that a literal book, a scroll of each person's life, rests in Heaven, written by God. What a fascinating thought! We can trust that God is writing a story from our life. He chose us uniquely for something special.

The Prophet Jeremiah's story is a perfect example of how God chooses us and develops a wonderful plan for our life:

> *"Before I _formed_ you in the womb I knew you,*
> *and before you were born I _consecrated_ you;*
> *I _appointed_ you a prophet to the nations."*
> **Jeremiah 1:5**

Note the underlined words above. Like Jeremiah we are <u>known</u> (loved and accepted), <u>consecrated</u> (prepared and made holy), and <u>appointed</u> (chosen for a purpose). God has chosen us.

God has a deliberate plan for your life. He knows where you live and what you need and has appointed you for something good. Acknowledge Him as the author of your story. Thank Him today for choosing you.

⸗ 5 ⸗

WE ARE HOLY
AND BLAMELESS
BEFORE GOD

"… that we should be <u>holy</u> and <u>blameless</u> before him…"
Ephesians 1:5

There is nothing like a bride on her wedding day. Women beam and exude confidence on this day perhaps more than any other day in their lives. Wedding ceremonies are full of beautiful symbolism and there is perhaps no greater event in the ceremony than when the bride walks down the aisle. In traditional weddings, brides wear white, symbolizing purity.

Having performed many weddings, as a pastor I'm often given a front row seat to this very special moment. The doors open, the music begins, and the bride begins her walk. Here, I always pay special attention not only to the bride, but also to the face of the groom. The love, acceptance, and absolute delight at seeing his future wife causes many a man to be overcome with emotion.

This is a beautiful moment because marriage is beautiful, and yet it's not simply the adornment and festivities of a wedding that emit this beauty. Marriage points us to a wedding of God to His people, described metaphorically in the book of Revelation. Revelation 21:2 says that at the end of time the church will appear before God as a "bride, beautifully dressed for her husband."

At the end of all time God's people, the church, will be like a bride, purified and prepared for her husband. Jesus will gaze upon His Bride and there will be no judgment, remorse, condemnation, or accusation in His eyes.

Reader, stop and think about this. When the King of Kings peers into you, He overlooks your faults to see your glory and your potential, like a bridegroom gazing upon a bride. God's love empowers us to fellowship with Him without condemnation or blame.

I've noticed this parallel in my work. As an employer of many engaged and newly married couples, it always makes me chuckle when I see a young couple canoodling in the front row of church, or distracted in a meeting while gazing in each other's eyes. Sometimes these young couples are so in love that they they are blind to the faults of their significant other. They see one another as "blameless."

Do you feel that the Lord looks that way towards you?

If you've ever felt that when God looks at you that He is displeased, or is quick to point out your faults, or sees you for your mistakes and hang-ups, it's time for a different understanding of God's nature. The Scriptures saw we stand "holy and blameless" before Him. How can this be?

We stand holy and blameless before God because of what Jesus has done for us. It's not that God doesn't see our sin - it's that He's dealt with it through Jesus. Like a bride walking down the aisle, full of grace and joy, we can approach God in confidence. Followers of Jesus can live by faith and enjoy life by the grace of God because we are forgiven.

Don't allow your identity to weakened by a misunderstanding of how God sees you. Refuse to let satan minimize your identity through condemnation and accusations. There is a great war for your identity. Our enemy works overtime to destroy our identity and accuse of of our weaknesses. This is why the Bible describes satan as the "accuser of the brethren" (Revelation 12:10).

God sees us as holy and blameless, pure and spotless. In some mysterious sense, we are His bride.

⸗ 6 ⸗

WE ARE ADOPTED
INTO GOD'S FAMILY

The Westminster Confession of Faith defines our adoption into God's family:

> *All those that are justified, God vouchsafes, in and for His only Son Jesus Christ, to make partakers of the grace of adoption, by which they are taken into the number, and enjoy the liberties and privileges of the children of God.*
> **The Westminster Confession of Faith**

As the Westminster Confession so aptly described, there is a parallel in our faith journey and the journey of adoption. There is something for us about the "liberties and privileges of the children of God."

> *"In love he predestined us for <u>adoption</u> to himself as sons through Jesus Christ…"*
> **Ephesians 1:5-6**

For many families the process of adopting a child can take months or years, ending legally when a judge pronounces the child as part of the new family. The end of the legal process, however, is just the beginning of the adoption story. The child and the family must learn how to bond together as the child is parented into a new way of life.

In a similar fashion, our spiritual adoption happens "legally" upon our salvation. When one becomes a follower of Jesus Christ, he or she is welcomed into God's family. This is the beginning of the identity journey.

> *"…but you have received the Spirit of adoption as sons, by whom we cry, "Abba! Father!" "*
> **Romans 8:15**

Much like the end of the legal process of adoption initiates a new season of parenting the adoptive child, our adoption into God's family begins a process of transformation in our life. Salvation, our adoption, is simply the beginning of our journey of discipleship.

The sad truth is that many Christians do not enjoy the *"liberties and privileges"* of being children of God. Although many have been legally adopted into God's family, most do not continue walking with God into deeper transformation. Just like an adopted child must learn the culture of his or her new family, developing the culture of the kingdom within us will take time.

Our new freedom in Jesus is real, but that freedom oftentimes does not abide in us without a fight. In order to receive the fullness of Christ's inheritance we must fight off old patterns that limit our God's ability to work in us.

> *"… throw off your old sinful nature and your former way of life…"*
> **Ephesians 4:22, NLT**

Just as an adopted child is legally part of his or her new family, but must spend time re-learning new habits and forgetting old ones, so we as Christians must learn the new way of operating as saints in the Kingdom of God. This process requires leaving habits, relationships, and beliefs that contrast the principles of God's family value system. God is after our transformation.

> *Do not be conformed to this world, but be transformed by the renewal of your mind, that by testing you may discern what is the will of God, what is good and acceptable and perfect.*
> **Romans 12:2**

Today, spend time identifying old patterns that are limiting you in your experience as a son or daughter of God. Where are mindsets or behaviors from your "former way of life," or perhaps unhealthy patterns from your family of origin, limiting your experience of God's Kingdom purposes?

≈ 7 ≈

WE ARE BELOVED
OF GOD AND IN THE
BELOVED OF GOD

"...he has <u>blessed</u> us in the <u>Beloved</u>..."
Ephesians 1:6

All Peoples Church, our church family in Southern California, has been graced by God to be a multi-ethnic and international church. Some counts have found that we have members in our church from over 50 countries, with a high percentage of our congregation being born out of the United States.

One special group in our church is a collection of families from Africa. These families moved to the United States as refugees. They left terrible circumstances in war-torn countries, lost everything, and were placed by our federal government in San Diego. We are so grateful that they became part of our church family.

In a recent meeting I was very impacted as a number of our African leaders sat in a circle and introduced themselves. I have found by studying how someone introduces his or herself you can learn a lot about a person's perception of their identity.

This collection of refugees did not share occupations, age, or status during their introductions. They simply identified themselves by their love for Jesus.

"My name is Jean Valle', and I love Jesus." "My name is Dorcas, and I love Jesus"
"My name is Oulouwa. It means 'flower.' And I love Jesus."

I was very impacted to hear about how these saints identified themselves. They wanted us to know that they loved Jesus… and that was enough.

We are God's beloved people.

Don't be deceived by defining yourself any other way. It is so tempting to define ourselves by our careers, family culture, origin, or hobbies. Circumstances, however, are a poor way to establish an identity.

These precious African believers have a faith that has been tested by unimaginable trials. And through that faith they have a unique revelation of God's love. They know they are God's beloved and their identity has been strengthened, not diminished, through fiery trials.

Circumstances, good or bad, were not meant to define us. It is only in knowing the love of God for ourselves, today, just as we are, that we are able to avoid the trappings of a lesser story.

Today, say your name aloud and declare your love for Jesus.

My name is Kendall, and I love Jesus.

Now, you: *"My name is _____. I love Jesus."*

Say it over and over again! Through your words you are defining yourself by love. You are *in God's beloved.*

≈ 8 ≈

WE HAVE BEEN REDEEMED AND FORGIVEN THROUGH HIS BLOOD

"In Him <u>we have redemption through his blood</u>, the forgiveness of our trespasses, according to the riches of his grace."
Ephesians 1:7

Many of the early Christians were from a Jewish background, and the readers of Ephesians were no exception. Jewish people have a special sense of being selected by God for a unique purpose because of their history as children of Abraham.

So, the Jewish reader of Ephesians would have taken special notice of the phrase "redemption through blood." This is a direct Biblical reference to the story of Passover.

What exactly *is* Passover? Described in Exodus 12, the Passover story is so significant that God turned the event into a holiday, commanding the Jewish people to remember it every year. The central theme of the Passover story is redemption through blood.

During Passover, God released judgment upon Egypt for the enslavement of the Hebrews. To spare His people from judgment, God gave them special instructions: take a lamb, kill it, have a family meal, and place the lamb's blood over their doorposts. He promised protection, stating:

"I am God. The blood will serve as a sign on the house where you live. When I see the blood I will pass over you - no disaster will touch you when I strike the land of Egypt."
Exodus 12:12-13 (MSG)

Passover is so named because death *passed over* the Hebrews on the way to Egypt. Because of the sign of the blood, the Hebrew people were spared. God didn't see the sin of Israel. Instead, He saw the blood. Judgment passed.

So, when Paul writes, "in him we have redemption through his blood" (Ephesians 1:4), the Jewish reader of Ephesians knows the subject well - the power of the blood. How does this relate to us today?

Just as a lamb was slain and its blood spread for the covering of God's people during Passover, Jesus's blood has been spread for us. Just as the destroyer over-looked the Jewish people because of that blood, so we have been saved from death and judgment for sin. We too have been passed over, because of the Lamb who took upon Himself the sins of the world.

"The next day he saw Jesus coming toward him, and said, "Behold, the Lamb of God, who takes away the sin of the world!"
John 1:29

Jesus is the Lamb of God who died to redeem your sins. Today, walk in freedom because the punishment for your sin fell on Jesus. When the Father sees His children He does not see people deserving of judgment - He sees people redeemed by blood.

Death has passed over God's people once more because of the blood of Christ. Meditate today on Jesus's blood as your redemption, for He was the perfect Passover Lamb.

'Saying with a loud voice, "Worthy is the Lamb who was slain, to receive power and wealth and wisdom and might and honor and glory and blessing!"'
Revelation 5:12

"… For Christ, our Passover lamb, has been sacrificed…"
1 Corinthians 5:7

⸗ 9 ⸗

WE HAVE LAVISHLY
RECEIVED GRACE

A number of years ago, U2 frontman, Bono, completed an interview with a rock and roll magazine. The interviewer, looking for an inside edge, was surprised and stunned as Bono began to speak about his faith in Jesus Christ. Bono's main point? "Grace over karma."

Let's look at his words below:

It's a mind-blowing concept that the God who created the universe might be looking for company, a real relationship with people, but the thing that keeps me on my knees is the difference between Grace and Karma… I really believe we've moved out of the realm of Karma into one of Grace… You see, at the center of all religions is the idea of Karma. You know, what you put out comes back to you: an eye for an eye, a tooth for a tooth, or in physics—in physical laws—every action is met by an equal or an opposite one. It's clear to me that Karma is at the very heart of the universe. I'm absolutely sure of it. And yet, along comes this idea called Grace to upend all that "as you reap, so you will sow" stuff. Grace defies reason and logic. Love interrupts, if you like, the consequences of your actions, which in my case is very good news indeed, because I've done a lot of stupid stuff…. That's between me and God. But I'd be in big trouble if Karma was going to finally be my judge… It doesn't excuse my mistakes, but I'm holding out for Grace. I'm holding out that Jesus took my sins onto the Cross, because I know who I am, and I hope I don't have to depend on my own religiosity.

I love Bono's words, "I'm holding out for grace." Grace sometimes sounds too good to be true but God has given it lavishly.

Consider today's passage:

> "...according to _the riches of his grace, which he has lavished_ upon us..."
> **Ephesians 1:7-8**

The word "grace" is mentioned in Ephesians 13 times.

It is primarily understand that we are rescued from sin by God's grace. Paul writes that grace provides us with salvation.

> "For by _grace_ you have been saved through faith. And this is not your own doing; it is the gift of God,"
> **Ephesians 2:8**

An often neglected aspect of grace is the empowerment it brings us to live on mission in our world. Grace provides us with a supernatural empowerment to serve and minister to others.

> "Of this gospel I was made a minister according to the gift of God's _grace_, which was given me by the working of his power."
> **Ephesians 3:7**

God treats us much better than we deserve. He has, through grace, given us a hope and a calling in Jesus Christ. We can leave our fear of failure and the confusion of religious performance behind. Instead, we can begin to walk in confidence as God's sons and daughters who will do the great works that God has prepared for them in advance.

Grace has been given lavishly to help us and others. Aren't you glad you don't get what you deserve (judgment) and grace instead?

Grace is certainly better than karma!

⚍ 10 ⚍

WE HAVE A PURPOSE

"making known to us the mystery of his will, according to his <u>purpose</u>, which he set forth in Christ."
Ephesians 1:9

"In him we have obtained an inheritance, having been predestined according to the <u>purpose</u> of him who works all things according to the counsel of his will..."
Ephesians 1:11

The "Purpose Driven Life," written by Pastor Rick Warren, is widely cited as being one of the greatest selling non-fiction books of all-time. In the introduction of his book, Warren writes:

"It's not about you. The purpose of your life is far greater than your own personal fulfillment, your peace of mind, or even your happiness. It's far greater than your family your career, or even your wildest dreams and ambitions. If you want to know why you were placed on this planet, you must begin with God. You were born by his purpose and for his purpose."
Rick Warren, The Purpose Driven Life

The success of Rick Warren's book lies in that God has used it to meet the simple need that He has placed in the hearts of all people: the need for purpose.

You might be surprised to learn that even outwardly "successful" people struggle with feeling a lack of purpose.

I have had the opportunity to meet with many successful leaders. I've met with business leaders, entrepreneurs, creative types, military leaders, and people pursuing public office. Here's what I've noticed: All types of people, regardless of their chosen path or profession, suffer from a degree of emptiness inside. Even people with a high degree of ambition can struggle with questions regarding destiny and purpose.

I remember one executive sharing with me that his entire career and life's work was worth nothing to him (this surprised me because he has amassed a large fortune and retired at the top of his field). His greatest advice to me? Make enough money to buy a vacation home. Then, he said, *you'll be happy.*
Isn't it ironic? Even the most envied people often live for the next grand vacation, the newest hobby, or some other way to escape their daily life. Many of us live under this same cloud of existential angst.

And yet, attaching yourself to the right purpose gives your life power. Purposeless breeds powerlessness, but when our lives are attached to the right purpose they are full of power, passion, and meaning.

This is what Jesus said about his life purpose, when questioned by the Ruler Pontius Pilate:

> *"You say that I am a king. For this <u>purpose</u> I was born and for this purpose I have come into the world—to bear witness to the truth."*
> **John 18:37**

Jesus was a leader that knew his purpose… and when we attach ourselves to His purposes, we have joy and vision for the task at hand.

Attach yourself today to the purpose of Jesus. You were born to serve His cause, not to build a kingdom of your own comfort. Declaring your purpose in Christ clears the fog of daily life that often clouds our vision. If you have success, thank God for it. If you have needs, bring them to God. When you choose to diligently seek our His purposes and not simply your own, He will work it out.

> *"And we know that God causes everything to work together for the good of those who love God and are called according to his <u>purpose</u> for them."*
> **Romans 8:28, NLT**

GOD HAS GIVEN YOU A UNIQUE PURPOSE.

≈ 11 ≈

WE KNOW
THE MYSTERY
OF GOD'S WILL

"He made known to us <u>the mystery of his will…</u>"
Ephesians 1:11

Have you ever felt that God's will for your life was a mystery?

Be encouraged: God has made know the mystery of His will to us in Christ.

I recall many late nights during my college years asking God big questions, things like:

"Who should I marry?"
"What should my major be? My job?"
"Should I become a pastor? A lawyer? A writer?"
"Where should I live after college?"

Many of us do not know what tomorrow brings practically for our lives. We all have questions about our path and struggle to determine the right steps to take for our future. Why is it that the Bible says, then, that we *already know* the mystery of God's will?

I have found that when I have faced questions regarding God's will in my life, my personal decisions are "micro-questions." It's not that these questions are not important. It's just that they are not primary. Our personal decisions are part of God's larger story of redemption and restoration.

When I resolved the "macro-question" of life's meaning by studying the big picture of God's will on earth, the rest of my life decisions started to fall in place. God has revealed the big picture of His will to us in Christ. When we get ahold of God's heart and God's purposes on earth, then the Holy Spirit is able to direct the particulars of our daily life.

Here's what Ephesians 1 says about the will of God:

The will of God…
+ was a mystery to the previous generations before Jesus.
+ has been made known to us.
+ was purposed in Christ.
+ will bring to unity everything in heaven and on earth,

The will of God is most typified in the attitude of Jesus demonstrated through what is known as "The Lord's Prayer." Jesus taught us to pray "Your Kingdom come, Your will be done, on earth as it is in Heaven" (Matt. 6:10).

Sometimes when we can't get the answer to a mystery in our life, we are asking the wrong question. We can get stuck on our "micro-questions." Rather than asking, "God…what is your will for my life?" ask, "*God what have you most created in me to bring your Kingdom to earth?*"

When I began to ask this question the journey became clear. Much like a boat getting into the current of a river, a desire to serve God and see His Kingdom touch others becomes a current of grace and generosity in our lives, pushing us to the next decision, the right location, and to important relationships.

> *"It's in Christ that we find out who we are and what we are living for."*
> **Ephesians 1:11, MSG**

God's purpose for our individual lives becomes clear when we see it in view of the greater picture of His desire to transform the world. Make a choice today to surrender your daily decisions to the current of the Kingdom. It will take you to the right place.

God, what have you most created me to do to bring your Kingdom to earth?

May you sense God's clarity in this request today.

⹀ 12 ⹀

WE HAVE AN INHERITANCE

"in Him we have obtained an <u>inheritance</u>…"
Ephesians 1:11

I have friends and acquaintances who have come of age and learned they possess the rights to a sizable financial inheritance. They were surprised when informed about the extent of their monetary trusts. Legally, one day previous generations will pass and that wealth will be theirs. They will have "obtained an inheritance."

The Bible declares that we too, as believers, have an inheritance. The concept of an inheritance is very important for Kingdom life because the metaphor describes how the promises of God apply to us as believers.

I've noticed several characteristics of people who learn that they will receive a sizable inheritance. Consider the parallels to spiritual life as you read.

✢ **People with an inheritance are risk-takers**

Recently Quartz Online re-published a study entitled *"Entrepreneurs don't have a special gene for risk—they come from families with money."* The findings from Ernst & Young and the Global Entrepreneurship Monitor interested me. Apparently, research demonstrates that most people who start businesses are backed by a large inheritance or financial nest egg provided by other family members. The thesis of the article was that this feeling of a "safety net" creates an environment for entrepreneurial risk.

In a similar fashion, our spiritual inheritance causes us to take risks for God's kingdom. Father God backs the steps of faith His children take.

✦ **People with an inheritance think generationally**

The Bible says "A good person leaves an inheritance for their children's children..." (Proverbs 13:22). By definition, an inheritance is something that is passed down from generation to generation.

Understanding that we have received an inheritance in Christ allows us to begin thinking about the generations of Kingdom people that have gone before us and those that will go after us. How will our decisions today affect the morality, the finances, the well-being, and the spiritual life of those that come after us? An inheritance is a great responsibility and healthy people who receive an inheritance have a desire to continue the blessing to further generations.

In God's Kingdom, we are called to think generationally. So much of Christian teaching concerning church life is temporal. Unfortunately, Christians can be just as self-focused and impatient as the rest of the population. But Psalm 145 says, "One generation commends your works to another; they tell of your mighty acts" (Psalm 145:4).

✦ **People with an inheritance have nothing to prove**

The Amplified Bible rephrases today's passage by saying *"in Him also we have received an inheritance [a destiny--we were claimed by God as His own]."*

An inheritance in Christ means that you have access to a significant family (God's) and a significant purpose (extending God's Kingdom). Although our world tempts us to compromise our identity by defining our self by temporal means, our identity in Christ allows us to stand confidently and securely in God's grace… regardless of our external situation.

Generational wealth tends to shape mindsets around the long-game. Because we have an inheritance we can stop looking for quick-fixes. God is a God of the long-run and seeds we plant today will shape the future for many people.

Your inheritance is guaranteed for all eternity in Jesus Christ. How might that affect your actions and attitude today?

⹀ 13 ⹀

WE ARE
THE PRAISE
OF HIS GLORY

"In him we have obtained an inheritance, having been predestined according to the purpose of him who works all things according to the counsel of his will, so that we who were the first to hope in Christ might be to <u>the praise of his glory.</u>"
Ephesians 1:11-12

What does it mean to be the *"praise of His glory?"*

Euphoria overtook me upon the birth of each of my children. Like every parent, I know that my children will make mistake and have imperfections... but in those few moments after their birth I was overtaken by pure joy. My children in those moments truly became the *praise of my glory.*

My love for my children is genuine, but it is also imperfect when compared to the love of a perfect Heavenly Father. God's love never fails.

"He will rejoice over you with joy; He will be quiet in His love [making no mention of your past sins], He will rejoice over you with shouts of joy."
Zephaniah 3:17 (Amplified Version)

"He will be quiet in His love - making no mention of your past sins!" This statement is almost shocking. Too often Christians are taught about what displeases God rather than what God praises... we are the praise of His glory!

Could it really be true that God does not hold our past sins against us? God's people are the praise of His Glory. How are we to handle our imperfections and sins in light of God's mercy?

To truly understand your identity in Christ you must learn how to separate your behavior and God's discipline from your right standing with God as His son or daughter. Even when your life does not reflect God's nature you are still the praise of His glory. God rejoices over you not because of your performance, but because of Christ's perfection.

God's acceptance and praise of us does not minimize our sin, it simply maximizes the power of the Cross. When we admit our brokenness we attract the grace of God. God does not distance Himself in displeasure. Instead, He brings transformation through discipline.

> *"My dear child, don't shrug off God's discipline, but don't be crushed by it either. It's the child he loves that he disciplines; the child he embraces, he also corrects. God is educating you; that's why you must never drop out. He's treating you as dear children. This trouble you're in isn't punishment; it's training, the normal experience of children."*
> **Romans 12:4:11 (MSG)**

Refuse to empower the lie that God's affections are changed by your own moral or religious performance. Instead, trust in the goodness of God and draw near to God, even when you sense God's discipline in your life regarding poor choices. There is no sense trying to manage your holiness in your own strength. Allow His kindness and mercy to lead you to a deep and true repentance (Romans 2:4).

Our belief that we displease God leads us to disqualify ourselves from experiencing God's presence. Nothing could be further from our true identity. Invite the Holy Spirit into your place of struggle today knowing that you are still, even in your fight, the praise of His glory.

> *"There is therefore now no condemnation for those who are in Christ Jesus."*
> **Romans 8:1**

> *"…where the Spirit of the Lord is, there is freedom."*
> **2 Corinthians 3:17**

WE ARE SEALED
WITH THE
HOLY SPIRIT

"In him you also, when you heard the word of truth, the gospel of your salvation, and believed in him, were sealed with the promised Holy Spirit, who is the guarantee of our inheritance until we acquire possession of it, to the praise of his glory."
Ephesians 1:13-14

A seal is permanent, powerful, and everlasting, leaving a permanent mark on a document, a building, or an institution. I recently learned about the *seal* and insignia used by Princeton University, an Ivy League college.

Princeton is one of the most prestigious universities in the world. Alumni include 2 presidents, 43 Nobel laureates, 12 supreme court justices, the CEOs of Google and Amazon, and many other prominent thinkers, artists, politicians, and societal influencers. Many people do not know, however, the spiritual history of this important institution.

Princeton was founded in 1746 as a training college for Christian ministers and has a rich history of dedication to God. The university's third president was Jonathan Edwards, a famous revivalist and pastor during the American Great Awakening. His ministry resulted in thousands of people coming to Christ, resulting in societal reformation across the American colonies.

Princeton itself was host to many revival meetings and has a rich prophetic history of moves of the Holy Spirit. It is an institution with an incredible spiritual heritage waiting to be recovered.

Although many recent graduates of Princeton have no idea of the spiritual history of the university there is an emblem that constantly reminds every student of God's call and destiny - the university seal.

The seal is marked with the historical university motto, *"Dei Sub Numine Viget,"* or, *"Under the Protection of God She Flourishes."* Any student of visitor to the campus of Princeton has the opportunity to uncover this radical promise because the university is sealed with a promise from God.

Spiritually speaking, we have been *sealed* with the Holy Spirit. We have an identity and a purpose that cannot be removed.

✤ **We are sealed with the Holy Spirit because we are God's possession.**

Much like an antique brand or coat of arms, a seal indicates ownership. We have been sealed with the Holy Spirit because through relationship with Jesus we are God's possession. One seals an important possession as a sign of ownership and belonging. God's permanent protection rests upon us because we belong to Him.

✤ **We are sealed with the Holy Spirit as a sign of God's promise.**

You may have heard the phrase, before *"to seal the deal."* A seal is a future promise of security and establishment. We have been "sealed" by the Holy Spirit as a guarantee, a down payment, of the eternal reward and fellowship we will receive through Christ in Heaven.

✤ **We are sealed with the Holy Spirit to mark us with purity.**

When you desire to protect a painted surface from the elements, you cover it with a *sealant*. A seal protects the purity of an object from outside forces. God's sealing you with the Holy Spirit is a mark of the purity He has given you in Christ. Regardless of your past mistakes or wrong doings, you have become the "righteousness of God" in Christ Jesus (2 Corinthians 5:21). You are a new creation.

You have been sealed with the Holy Spirit. You can trust the work of the Holy Spirit in your life. Know that God desires to protect you as His sealed possession, that you may flourish.

UNDER THE PROTECTION OF GOD YOU WILL FLOURISH.

= 15 =

WE HAVE A
HEAVENLY FATHER

"the <u>Father</u> of Glory…"
Ephesians 1:17

The presence of a father in the home is one of the most statistically significant indicators of academic achievement, emotional welfare, and financial success of children. Tragically we live in a day and age where many people grow up in a family system in which their father is abusive, unavailable, or absent. Secular and sacred voices agree on the fact that fatherlessness is greatly damaging our society. In one lucid Washington Post op-ed, a Pulitzer Prize awarded social scientist pronounced that *"Fatherlessness is America's Single Largest Source of Poverty."*

God has an answer for this pain. By God's grace you can "beat the odds" of familial brokenness by experiencing the security and safety of knowing your *Heavenly Father.*

One leader in the Bible who was forced to overcome a difficult relationship with his father was King David. In Psalm 51 David writes, "in sin, my mother conceived me." Bible scholars believe that this passage indicates that David was an illegitimate child. As we read through David's leadership journey , it's obvious that something was "off" about his family of origin. Why is out he tending the sheep when the prophet Samuel comes around? Why does Jesse, David's father, neglect and ignore him so openly? David knew the pain that comes from not belonging even in one's own family.

> *"So he asked Jesse, "Are these all the sons you have?" "There is still the youngest," Jesse answered. "He is tending the sheep…"*
> **1 Samuel 16:11 NIV**

Painfully, David also ends up rejected by his spiritual father, Saul. It is sad to see that many people carry wounds inflicted upon them not only by their earthly fathers, but also by spiritual leaders.

Yet, in the midst of this pain, David declares, "my father and mother walked out on me, but the Lord took me in" (Psalm 27:10, MSG). David, like all of us, had to experience the love and acceptance of his Heavenly Father in order to live a healthy life. We have a heavenly Father.

Consider this acronym of the word *"FATHER"* as you meditate on the goodness of your Heavenly Father today.

Faithful   God your Heavenly Father is *faithful* to you. His word never returns void (Isaiah 55:10). He is good on all His promises.

Available   God your Heavenly Father is *available*. You are His priority. He responds quickly when He hears your call and has plenty of time to listen to you.

Teacher   God your Heavenly Father is a *teacher*. Many of us feel like we have no one to guide us in our families, our careers, or regarding practical life needs. He will make sure you know what you need to know and lead you to good success.

Healer   God your Heavenly Father is a *healer*. He desires to heal you… however needed - spirit, soul, or body. He "heals up the brokenhearted" (Psalm 147:3).

Encourager   God your Heavenly Father is an *encourager*. If you quiet your heart to hear His voice you will hear His encouraging affirmation. God is on your side.

Righteous   God your Heavenly Father is *righteous*. The disappointment or pain you have received from your own father or from other leaders does not reflect God's heart for you. God will always treat you with purity and respect. You can trust His plans and goodwill for your life.

"See how very much our Father loves us, for he calls us his children…"
1 John 3:1 NLT

= 16 =

WE HAVE
WISDOM

"...that the God of our Lord Jesus Christ, the Father of glory, may give you the Spirit of <u>wisdom</u> and of revelation in the knowledge of him..."
Ephesians 1:17

Think for a moment of the stories, the movies, or the books that have touched your heart and shaped your life. Many of these stories share common elements and themes that appeal to the universal human condition.

Psychologists and anthropologists note that impacting stories share a similar form with frequently repeated iconic characters. Stories have heroes, villains, comic relief characters, love interests, and *guides*.

The guide plays an important role in our favorite stories. A great tale always includes a great adventure, and to succeed in his or her epic quest the hero requires the leadership of a guide. Dante had Virgil, Frodo had Gandalf, Luke Skywalker had Obi-Wan, Neo had Morpheus, and even Simba had Rafiki! The need for a guide is universal to all people. And what a guide primarily supplies is *wisdom*.

We need a guide because we need wisdom. This is the reason the self-help industry generates millions of dollars a year. It's why we consume podcasts, attend seminars, and even why we look on "Yelp" before visiting a new restaurant.

Who is the guide in your own story? Who will equip you for your destiny? Who will lead you from darkness of ignorance into wisdom's glorious light?

God has provided you in your story with the most reliable Guide, the Holy Spirit, described in Ephesians as the "spirit of wisdom and revelation."

Jesus promised that the Holy Spirit would guide us into "all truth."

> *"When the Spirit of truth comes, he will guide you into all the truth…"*
> **John 16:13**

In Christ we have an expert guide that will *always* be available to give us the wisdom we need. That guide is the Holy Spirit.

It may be that a human "guide" or mentor has yet to appear in your life because God is waiting for you to discover the Heavenly Guide that He has already written into your story. Perhaps God is taking you where others have not been. Make a choice today to rely on God as your source of wisdom.

As you make your life choices, choose wisdom. Avoid running after fads, money, or the opinions of others. God will give you wisdom when you ask, and through wisdom you will receive everything you need.

> *Blessed is the one who finds wisdom, and the one who gets understanding, for the gain from her is better than gain from silver and her profit better than gold.*
> **Proverbs 4:6-8**

Listed below are a few admonitions that the Biblical proverbs give concerning wisdom:

+ Fear, honor, and revere God. This is the beginning of wisdom (Proverbs 1:7, 9:10).

+ When God gives you wisdom, treasure it (Proverbs 2:1, 3:21, 5:1).

+ Wisdom comes to the humble (Proverbs 11:2, 28:6).

+ Listen to the instruction of wise people and parents in your life (Proverbs 13:1, 15:22). God has put them there for a reason.

If you are a follower of Jesus Christ you already have access to all the wisdom you need because you have the Holy Spirit. God is your guide.

≈ 17 ≈

WE HAVE
REVELATION

" ...that the God of our Lord Jesus Christ, the Father of glory, may give you the Spirit of wisdom and of <u>revelation</u> in the knowledge of him..."
Ephesians 1:17

All relationships are based upon communication and God certainly wants to communicate with us. Throughout the Scriptures we see that relationship with God is based upon direct, personal communication. Adam communed with God in the garden. Abraham followed a voice. Joseph received spiritual dreams. The Holy Spirit spoke and led the early church. God is One who speaks and reveals His perfect nature to imperfect people.

Sadly, many Christians today struggle with "revelation," the belief that we are able to hear and receive personally from God. And yet, the Scriptures promise a God who is "not silent" (Psalm 50:3). Jesus said it this way:

"Whoever belongs to God hears what God says..."
John 8:47

Whoever belongs to God hears what God says. It is amazing to me that hearing God's voice is not a privilege for a few extra-special Christians. Instead, receiving revelation from God is the birthright of every believer. Just as any infant can discern the voice of his or her parent, we have been hard-wired and designed as children of the Lord to hear His voice.

I have found that God takes many people through a process of development in learning to hear His voice. Much like learning a foreign language, discerning the meaning of what God might be saying to you is a process. Think about it in the context of studying a foreign language:

+ **It takes time to learn God's language.**

Just like acquiring a foreign language requires time and patience, learning to receive revelation from God is a process. This is why the Scriptures implore us to "wait" on the Lord (Psalm 5:3). God allows this process because His primary goal is deeper relationship with us.

+ **God's language has a different vocabulary.**

Whereas humans are familiar with literal speech and writing, God reveals Himself to us in many ways. The Bible says that the heavens "pour forth speech" and "night after night reveal knowledge" (Psalm 19:2). God rarely speaks to us in overt, human terms. Instead, He speaks in creative means. God's vocabulary is a vocabulary of symbols used in dreams, in nature, in impressions, and through feelings. God speaks through our relationships and through the Bible.

+ **God has provided us a wonderful "translation book."**

The Bible fully encapsulates God's truth and is the standard for faith and practice for all believers. Our hearing from God is not flaky or fleeting - it is built upon the foundation of the Scriptures. Our desire to hear from the Lord must drive us to what He has already spoken in the Scriptures. This is where we find context for the individual revelation God is speaking to us. The Bible is the best place to begin your process of hearing from God and every revelation from God must be tested by Scripture. Scripture cannot be broken (John 10:35).

+ **The best way to learn God's language is "immersion."**

When we read the book of Acts we see that God intended the church to be a place where His voice was frequently discerned. As the church gathered it is written that "The Holy Spirit said..." (Acts 13:2). When we are immersed in a community of healthy believers we are in a place to discover God's language for us. The wisdom, faith, and encouragement of others enables us to further receive from God.

Don't give up in your journey of trying to listen to God. It is part of the Christian's birthright. If you belong to God you can hear what He says.

= 18 =

WE HAVE
EYES THAT SEE
WHAT GOD IS DOING

"I pray that <u>the eyes of your heart</u> may be enlightened in order that you may know the hope to which he has called you…"
Ephesians 1:18

I have a child whose vision requires glasses. I will never forget the day we realized this as parents - and the day after he received his first pair. Every aspect of his development, confidence, and personality seemed to skyrocket when his vision became clear. In a similar way, having clear spiritual vision is essential to our growth as believers.

Vision produces clarity. This is not simply a physical principle, but also a spiritual one. When we received God's "glasses," life becomes clear.

Imagine, then, the significance of what Paul writes in Ephesians when he prays for the early church. The Passion Translation interprets today's passage as follows:

"I pray that the light of God will illuminate the eyes of your imagination, flooding you with light, until you experience the full revelation of the hope of his calling—that is, the wealth of God's glorious inheritances that he finds in us, his holy ones!"
Ephesians 1:18, PT

It may be hard to believe, but getting a picture of what God is doing in your life is easy… because seeing what God is doing is part of your identity in Jesus Christ. Because of Jesus, we can have a clear sense of what God is doing in our life.

The verse above highlights three important keys to understanding what God is doing in your life.

✛ **Spiritual perception**

God gives us a means spiritual perception, the "eyes of the heart,"to discern what He is doing in our life. Sadly, like the child who needs glasses, many people do not see the world correctly because of pain, trauma, and false beliefs. Our painful experiences cloud our ability to receive revelation from God.

Don't feel condemned if you are struggling to perceive what God is doing in your life. It's encouraging to know that even prophets experience times where their spiritual perception is just *off*. David, Elijah, and Jeremiah all recount battles with despair and loneliness in the Scriptures.

Sin, brokenness, and despair can distort our spiritual perception. Jesus warned His followers during the famous Sermon on the Mount about this reality. "If then the light within you is darkness, how great is that darkness!" (Matthew 6:23). We cannot see what God is doing in our life when we are filled with darkness.

As a pastor I have often met with people who are struggling to find God's will for their lives. It is of no surprise to me that the people with the least vision and who typically feel the most distant from God have some kind of unconfessed sin, trauma, or brokenness. Darkness and light cannot coexist. Keep a short account with God.

To fully claim the promise that you can see what God is doing in your life, be sure that you are pursuing healing, forgiveness, and deliverance from past hurts, hang-ups, and brokenness. You will find that as you experience freedom in Christ that your spiritual perception becomes clear.

✤ Spiritual atmosphere

Painters, sculptors, and other fine artists are aware of the importance of different types of light. It is commonly known that natural north-facing light is the best light in which to produce a painting. It is in this setting that light is most consistent throughout the course of a day. Eastward or westward facing windows vary in illumination due to the rising and setting of the sun. In northern light, however, the quality of light does not change during a day in the artist's studio.

The quality of light affects our ability to see. Interestingly, there is a spiritual light the Scripture speaks of that also influences how we perceive the world. The Psalmist writes of the "light of God's face."

"Blessed are the people who know the festal shout, who walk, O Lord, in the light of your face..."
Psalm 89:15

God's light is an important theme in Scripture. Paul prays that the eyes of our heart be "enlightened" or as the Passion Translation describes it, "illuminated." This metaphor of light speaks of the presence of God.

Just like the north-facing light is the best light in which to paint, the light of God's face is the best light in which to consider your life. It is very hard to get a picture of God's will for your life by looking at yourself, through your own light. Introspection typically leads us to pride or condemnation. When we look at Jesus we see a light without reflection or shifting shadow. In Jesus' light everything becomes clear.

Remove yourself from places that have a spiritual atmosphere which brings confusion or despair regarding what God is doing in your life. Look at Jesus to create the right spiritual atmosphere in your life to hear from God. He is your guiding light.

✤ Spiritual attitude

My father often quotes the words of Zik Ziglar, motivational speaker, who famously stated *"your attitude is your altitude."* In a similar way, your revelation of God's goodness will be proportional to your level of hope (your spiritual attitude).

Paul writes that God wants to reveal the "hope to which he has called us." As you ask God to show you what is going on in your life, know that God wants to leave you in a place of hope.

"May the God of hope fill you with all joy and peace in believing, so that by the power of the Holy Spirit you may abound in hope."
Romans 15:13

Amazingly, the Bible says that God will actually exceed our imaginations in showing us His goodness. "He is able to do immeasurably more than all we ask or imagine" (Ephesians 3:20).

As God transforms your spiritual perception, changes your spiritual atmosphere, and improves your spiritual attitude, you will perceive His will more clearly. Spend time each day asking God for wisdom and asking Him to show you, in your imagination, what He is doing in your life. Write down what you feel, sense, or see.

⹀ 19 ⹀

WE HAVE
THE HOPE
OF HIS CALLING

"… in order that you may know the hope to which he has called you…"
Ephesians 1:18

Victor Frankl, in his autobiographical account of survival as a Jewish doctor during the horrors of the WWII Holocaust, made a startling observation about the power of hope. In that crushing environment, Frankl observed the extraordinary power of people to withstand all kinds of pressures. Despite illness, abuse, neglect, and starvation, Frankl observed that hope, above all else, had the power to keep men alive.

It is true that hope brings life. This spiritual principle is essential to understand if you desire to be a person of prayer. To pray effectively, fervently, and with longevity, one must be a person of hope.

God knows about our need for hope. Research has shown Jeremiah 29:11 consistently ranks amongst the top 5 quoted Bible verses in our culture today. This verse describes God's plan to give us gives "a hope and a future". Ephesians 1 declares we have been "called," called to hope. We have a hope and therefore a calling.

Victor Frankl sought to make his life mission giving hope to others. Based upon his experience in the concentration camp, he developed a new form of therapy for hurting people, called *logotherapy*. Frankl believed that helping a person find meaning in their life could help them find hope. To Frankl, when one finds meaning, her or she will find hope.

It is noble and powerful how Frankl used transformed his pain and trauma to make a difference in the lives of others. I was deeply impacted by reading Frankl's work. Yet, I was struck with a distinction between Frankl's perspective and what Jesus has to offer.

Every human requires meaning in life, but as followers of Jesus our hope comes from a higher source. We do not have hope because we have personal meaning. We have a calling and a future *because we have hope.*

For us, hope comes first. Our hope is not found in our own search for meaning or in own life's work. Our hope comes through the death, burial, resurrection, and ascension of Jesus Christ.

When we understand the hope we have in Jesus Christ's finished work on the cross - that we have a hope that is secure beyond our own performance, emotions, abilities, or passions - hope becomes alive. Part of our identity in Christ is that we possess a living hope. One example of such hope in the Bible is the hope of Abraham, who believed for child and an inheritance in impossible circumstances.

> *"When everything was hopeless, Abraham believed anyway, deciding to live not on the basis of what he saw he couldn't do but on what God said he would do."*
> **Romans 4:18, MSG**

When we feel like giving up, we still have a hope. When life and suffering provides no meaning, we still have hope. And yes, there are times in life when our calling and own search for meaning provides us with motivation - but when we have nothing else, we *still* have hope because of what Jesus did for us.

We are called to carry the living hope of Jesus Christ.

> *"Praise be to the God and Father of our Lord Jesus Christ! In his great mercy he has given us new birth into a living hope through the resurrection of Jesus Christ from the dead."*
> **1 Peter 1:3**

≂ 20 ≂

WE HAVE
GLORIOUS RICHES

"… the <u>riches of his glorious inheritance</u> in the saints…"
Ephesians 1:18

In the movie "National Treasure," the protagonist Ben Gates (Nicholas Cage), fueled by his patriotism and spirit of adventure, embarks on an epic treasure hunt of historical significance. The movie ends (spoiler alert!) with Gates and his crew discovering a massive ancient treasure under Trinity Church in New York City, just one block from the Wall Street Stock Exchange.

Although I doubt Disney intended this, the end of this movie has prophetic significance for those of us on an identity journey.

Wall Street symbolizes how we often view success in worldly terms. The *Trinity Church* depicts the Kingdom of God. The *riches* under the church are a sign of the massive resources that God desires to make available to us. Much like in the film, divine resources are often hidden, delayed, or only available to those who seek after them.

I love the contrast the movie presents between Wall Street (where we expect wealth and power to rest) and the hidden riches beneath Trinity Church. To me the symbols poses us a question. Where will we look for our provision? Through God's Kingdom… or through the systems of this world?

It is easy to look at the riches, influence, and prestige of society and be impressed. However, don't be deceived however and confuse riches and status for spiritual maturity. The world does not have abundant supply and there is no glory in its riches. Although we are to honor those who work hard with excellence and integrity, financial stewardship is really just a training ground for the stewardship that we believers have of the Kingdom of God.

Consider these words of Jesus:

> *"And if you are untrustworthy about worldly wealth, who will trust you with the true riches of heaven?"*
> **Luke 16:11, NLT**

Much like Ben Gates in the movie "National Treasure", we must look beyond Wall Street to meet our needs and be our supply. There are true riches available to us, hidden in plain sight, when we pursue the Kingdom of God. God has called us to become *Kingdom Treasure Hunters* that pursue the glorious riches made available to us in Christ Jesus.

> *"I will give you the treasures of darkness and the hoards in secret places, that you may know that it is I, the Lord, the God of Israel, who call you by your name."*
> **Isaiah 45:3 ESV**

What treasures may the Lord have hidden for you during this identity journey?

"I WILL GIVE YOU THE TREASURES OF DARKNESS..."

21

WE HAVE
GOD'S POWER
WORKING TOWARDS US

"… and what is the immeasurable greatness of his power toward us who believe, according to the working of his great might…"
Ephesians 1:19

A *pilgrimage* is a journey of spiritual significance.

Pilgrimage has a long history amongst followers of God. In the Old Testament the Hebrew people found themselves on a spiritual journey through the Wilderness towards the Promised Land. Pilgrimages to Jerusalem began when the the temple was rebuilt, 900 years before Christ. The Psalmist writes of a pilgrimage journey to climb the Temple Mount, asking "Who shall ascend the hill of the LORD? And who shall stand in his holy place?" (Psalm 24:3).

Pope Benedict writes:

"To go on pilgrimage is not simply to visit a place to admire its treasures of nature, art or history. To go on pilgrimage really means to step out of ourselves in order to encounter God where he has revealed himself…"

Some pilgrimages begin with intention, like a tour of the Holy Land. Other journeys are spontaneously directed by the Lord, such as when the disciples walked on the Road to Emmaus. Either way, we see through Scripture and experience that God will often take His people on a physical journey to encourage spiritual transformation. In many ways, our lives are a pilgrimage.

God directed me on a spontaneous pilgrimage during my university years while studying abroad in London. Here, I became aware for the first time of the "immeasurable greatness of his power."

The journey began with a time of prayer one morning. I felt directed by the Holy Spirit to take a train that weekend to Oxford, England. Oxford is about a two hour train ride from London.

I visited Oxford and explored Blackwell's Books, the Eagle and the Child pub, and finally, Christ Church. While sitting in Christ Church Cathedral I began to feel the presence of God. This was the destination of my pilgrimage.

In prayer I felt the Holy Spirit direct me to the bookstore of the large cathedral. I walked into the bookstore and in the back-right-corner of the store saw a small, purple book. God spoke to my heart, saying, "that's why I sent you here." The small purple book was titled "The Fire of the North: The Life of St. Cuthbert." It had a sacred, mystical feeling about it. I purchased it and got ready to take the train back to London.

Over the next few days I read that book three times. It was the jewel of my pilgrimage to Oxford, the gift of encounter that God had hidden there for me. I read about this man who is known as "Cuthbert of Lindisfarne."

Cuthbert (634 - 687 AD) served God's people as a monk, a bishop, an evangelist, a pastor, and a friend. The most notable thing about Cuthbert's life, however, was his experience of the power of God. Cuthbert's legacy was to be known as the "Wonder Worker of England."

As I read Cuthbert's life story it was as if an entire aspect of the Christian faith became clear to me - "the immeasurable greatness of his power towards us who believe." I read about the healings, the visions, the prophecies, the miracles, and the supernatural occurrences that surrounded Cuthbert's life.

I learned how many of these miracles were recorded by the Venerable Bede amongst his otherwise dry "Ecclesiastical History of the English People." I read about the Celtic Church, a group of Irish and Scottish believers whom from 300-700 AD were responsible for the re-evangelization of Europe through arts, storytelling, and the power of God. I became fascinated and determined to see God's power in my life, too.

Upon my second reading of the book I filled the margins of the small text with notes, Biblical references, and my own commentary.

I knew that this revelation was a special gift from God. This man, Cuthbert, had been used in amazing ways to bring the power of God to his generation. *"Could God do something like that again?"* I wondered… could God's power be working towards me?

Reflecting on the Scriptures, I turned to James chapter 5:

> *"The prayer of a righteous man is powerful and effective. Elijah was a man just like us. He prayed earnestly that it would not rain, and it did not rain on the land for three and a half years…*
> ***James 5:16-18 (NIV 1984)***

I wrote in the back of that book something like this:

> *"ELIJAH was a man just like me…"*

And I prayed something like this…

> *"God, you didn't love Elijah any more than you loved me. You said that the prayer of a righteous man is powerful and effective. My prayers do not feel powerful and effective… but I thank you that I have been made righteous by the blood of Jesus Christ. I am the righteousness of God in Christ Jesus. Will you fill me with your great power?"*

And then, again writing in the back of the book, I wrote this:

> *"CUTHBERT was a man just like me…"*

God brought me on a pilgrimage, a spiritual journey, to teach me about the "greatness of his power towards us who believe." Shortly after this experience is when I began to experience the power of God. I realized that I have God's power working towards me.

There is nothing particularly unique about St. Cuthbert, except that he was a man that was used by God. Elijah did not have a special spiritual pedigree either. He was a man, just like us. God uses ordinary people to display His extraordinary power.

Experiencing the power of God towards us is required for the power of God to work through us. When we experience God's power for ourselves we become, as one translation describes it, an "advertisement" for God's power to the world… much like Cuthbert.

> *"I pray that you will continually experience the immeasurable greatness of God's power made available to you through faith. Then your lives will be an advertisement of this immense power as it works through you!"*
> **Ephesians 1:19 TPT**

An amazing revelation regarding our identity in Christ is that God's power is working towards us. We can trust in the power of God not because of our own right standing with God but because of the righteous identity we received in Jesus Christ.

Choose today to begin your own pilgrimage in search of the power of God.

BE A PILGRIM

IN SEARCH OF THE

POWER OF GOD.

22

WE HAVE CHRIST AS OUR HEAD

"And God placed all things under his feet and <u>appointed him to be head over everything</u> for the church, which is his body, the fullness of him who fills everything in every way."
Ephesians 1:22-23

When we describe someone as our "head" we are saying that they are our "chief," "principal," and "leader." Jesus is head over everything and deserving of our worship and respect. What then, does it mean practically to approach the Lord with an attitude of submission and surrender?

Pastor Nicky Gumbel of Holy Trinity Brompton recounts this story about submission to Christ:

In London's National Gallery hangs a fifteenth-century Renaissance painting by Italian Filipino Lippi. The painting, titled *"The Virgin and Child with Saints Jerome and Dominic,"* depicts the Mother Mary tenderly holding the Jesus, as a child, on her lap. The anachronistic onlookers of this classic Virgin and Child scene are saints Dominic and Jerome. They are kneeling in worship.

Robert Cumming, an art critic with an exemplary reputation, was confused by the painting. Lippi was a well known Renaissance artist and the painting was worth hanging in London's gallery simply due to its place in history. Lippi was an expert painter with a command of his craft by using color, composition, and contrast masterfully.

Many visitors of the gallery commented that the painting was simply awkward. The proportions were skewed. The hills in the background seemed exaggerated. The subjects seemed to be seated in painful, uncomfortable positions. Journalist Robert Cumming pondered the painting, his inner critic dissecting technical issues of perspective and form.

As Cumming pensively studied the work it occurred to him that the painting was originally an altarpiece, commissioned for a wealthy Italian family. The painting had never been intended to hang in a gallery but instead was designed for prayer, reflection, and confession. So, to view the painting in its original form, the story goes that the respected Robert Cumming *fell upon his knees* in that world class art museum right in the middle of London's Covent Garden.

Next, everything came into perspective. Robert Cumming was looking at the painting as the artist intended. The awkward composition fell into place. The painting, rather than exuding a stifling and awkward feeling, began to bring Cumming reverence and inspiration.

This story beautifully illustrates what happens in our life when we begin to view Christ as our head. Many people do not have the right perspective of Jesus Christ. They stare at Him as a man, assuming equality with His nature. Others prefer to study Jesus's works and words but do not bow their hearts to Him in reverence. When we approach God with a human perspective, on our terms and not His, we are bound to end up with a poor understanding of His nature.

However, when we, like Robert Cumming, get on our knees before God, everything changes. The Kingdom becomes clear when we approach Jesus in an attitude of submission and humility, with what the Desert Fathers called *poverty of spirit*.

Worship and submission is the right approach in our hearts towards God and experiencing His nature. One aspect of understanding our identity in Christ is the decision to consistently make Jesus our leader, our head. Your identity is in the right place when your heart is submitted to Him.

It's true. Kneeling before Jesus brings everything into perspective.

KNEELING

BEFORE JESUS

PUTS EVERYTHING

INTO PERSPECTIVE.

≈ 23 ≈

WE ARE
CHRIST'S BODY

Ephesians 1 defines the church as "his body."

> *"…which is his <u>body</u>, the fullness of him who fills all in all…"*
> **Ephesians 1:23**

The Church is the body of Christ. This is an important spiritual truth, but what does it mean practically? In order to fully understand God's plan for the church to be Christ's "body," let's explore the way the Body of Christ is portrayed in the Gospels:

+ **The Body of Christ is born of the Holy Spirit**

  Jesus's physical body arrived on earth through a miracle, the Virgin Birth. Jesus, as the Apostle's Creed dictates, was "conceived by the Holy Spirit." Spiritually speaking, Christ's followers are also born of the Holy Spirit. We are *born again t*hrough the Spirit of God.

  We must remember that as followers of Jesus we have the Holy Spirit within us. Christianity is not simply just a worldview of principles - it is spiritual life born of the Holy Spirit. What is born of the Holy Spirit God intends to sustain through the work of the Holy Spirit. Christ's body receives its life not from self-strength, but from the very spirit of God.

+ **The Body of Christ is supernatural.**

  Jesus performed many miracles with His physical body. He turned water into wine, cleansed lepers, cast out evil spirits, and walked on water… all while constrained in the boundaries of human flesh. The Church is also called to walk in the supernatural power of the Spirit.

Whenever the church gathers we should expect God to be healing the sick, changing lives through prophecy, and bringing spiritual freedom to those in bondage. The Body of Christ is supernatural.

✤ **The Body of Christ suffers for others.**

Just as Jesus bore the sins, shame, and pain of the world in His body on the tree (2 Peter 2:24), the Church is called to bear the burdens of the world. It is not easy to lead others, make disciples, or serve those in poverty. Foreign missions is expensive and complicated. Some nations persecute those who spread the message of Jesus.

We are called to suffer for others so that they may know Christ. We are an in-the-flesh example of the sacrifice Jesus made for all people.

"Now I rejoice in what I am suffering for you, and I fill up in my flesh what is still lacking in regard to Christ's afflictions, for the sake of his body, which is the church."
Colossians 1:24

✤ **The Body of Christ will be resurrected and glorified**

Jesus ends His earthly ministry by ascending into Heaven. He went there to prepare a place for us in eternity (John 14:2-3). Our permanent home is in Heaven.

Although we may suffer as Christians, God will never abandon His promise of eternal communion and reward. Never forget that as a Christian you will enjoy the glories and rewards of Heaven. You will have the hope-filled expectation of hearing Jesus say: "I am making everything new!" (Revelation 21:5).

Consider these words of Eugene Peterson from the Message Bible.

"The church is Christ's body, in which he speaks and acts, by which he fills everything with his presence."

How can God use you to fill the world with His Presence today?

THE CHURCH IS CHRIST'S BODY... BY WHICH HE FILLS EVERYTHING WITH HIS PRESENCE.

⸗ **24** ⸗

WE HAVE
RECEIVED
CHRIST'S FULLNESS

"And God placed all things under his feet and appointed him to be head over everything for the church, which is his body, <u>the fullness of him who fills everything in every way</u>."
Ephesians 1:22-23

The Bible contains a progressive unveiling of God's message of restoration. This message peaks with the "New Covenant," a revelation of the fullness of God in Jesus Christ. Now, we have everything we need in Christ to accomplish His will on earth.

Jesus has provided. Physically and emotionally you will always have needs but spiritually you have been given what you need in Christ. We have been filled by Him, with Him, *and* with His *authority*.

"For in him the whole fullness of deity dwells bodily, <u>and you have been filled in him</u>, who is the head of all rule and authority"
Colossians 2:9-10

It is an amazing thought to ponder, that we have *been filled in* him. Now, rather than simply asking and praying for the fullness of God, we are able to *start demonstrating* the power of God through words and actions to a hurting world. God has already given us His fullness.

What's the purpose of this filling from God? We have been given fullness to distribute, for God desires to fill "everything in every way."

Practically, God "fills everything in every way" through believers who are activated in the divine power that the Scriptures describe. This happens practically through our daily life - in our neighborhoods, family gatherings and in our workplaces. Every aspect of our lives matter and will be used to advance God's Kingdom. We are natural and supernatural people, on mission to see the world aflame with the glory of God.

Consider these words of Jesus:

> *"Truly, truly, I say to you, whoever believes in me will also do the <u>works</u> that I do; and greater <u>works</u> than these will he do…"*
> **John 14:12**

Jesus defines the works *we* will do as the works *He did*. That work and task is summarized elsewhere by the Apostle John.

> *The reason the Son of God appeared <u>was to destroy the works of the devil</u>.*
> **1 John 3:8**

The message is clear - we will do the work that Jesus did, destroying the devil's work and bringing transformation to a world that is decaying from the curse of sin. That's good news!

Practically, our *daily work* is meant to be transformed into Jesus's *greater works.* God will use His people, on mission in society, to "fill everything in every way."

Digging deeper, a quick study of the Greek word, "works," in John 14 sheds light for us in the modern day. The word used in John 14:12, *"ergon,"* is the word used for: *"task," "business,"* and *"employment."*

Christ lives in us and heals others through and in our God-designed vocations, career choices, and talents. We have received Christ's fullness in order to fill the world with His Presence. Our demonstration of the Kingdom in our vocation is part of the *"greater work"* that Christ prophesied. Regardless of the nature or place of your day-to-day employment the calling on your life is to destroy the work of the evil one by demonstrating the greater works of Jesus.

Many believers struggle with practically applying advice about being an ambassador for Christ in their secular workplaces. As a young adult I received excellent advice from a seasoned missionary about how to demonstrate God's love to those around me in a marketplace context. The leader spoke to me about *consistency, celebration, and crisis.*

+ Consistency - Be consistently available to the people you work with. Consistently pray for them and offer to pray with them. Demonstrate the fruit and the gifts of the Holy Spirit overtly as part of your natural lifestyle.

+ Celebration - Be a celebrator of people. Encourage them on their birthdays and remember important life events. God's kindness through you will often open others to the message of Jesus.

+ Crisis - Be available when people you know experience crises. It is during these vulnerable times in life when people are most open to transformation and feel most acutely their need for God's love.

Believers that work in various spheres of society are responsible for transforming the arena in which they serve. Think of the Biblical examples of Joseph, Daniel, Esther, and Solomon. These are all examples of leaders who chose to use their natural leadership gifts and talents to bring transformation to the society around them. Today, spheres of society such as business, government, education, science, media, art, and medicine are the arenas in which God wants to demonstrate His power to the world.

To know you have the fullness of Christ is to believe that God has given you everything you need to complete your divine assignment. Your daily work, though sometimes small and monotonous, will produce great fruit in the long-run because God is involved.

> *"One of the next great moves of God is going to be through the believers in the workplace."*
> **Billy Graham**

Experience and receive the fullness of His Presence today! Whether your daily work feels impossible or mundane - God will use it to expand His kingdom. Through your work and His work in you He desires to "fill everything in every way."

⚞ 25 ⚟

WE ARE
LOVED WITH
A GREAT LOVE

"As for you, you were dead in your transgressions and sins, in which you used to live when you followed the ways of this world and of the ruler of the kingdom of the air, the spirit who is now at work in those who are disobedient. All of us also lived among them at one time, gratifying the cravings of our flesh and following its desires and thoughts. Like the rest, we were by nature deserving of wrath But because of his great love for us, God, who is rich in mercy, made us alive with Christ even when we were dead in transgressions—it is by grace you have been saved."
Ephesians 2:1-5

We are loved with a great love.

When people learn of a God that loves them in a radical, reckless, and affectionate way they seem to pause and ask "could God really be that good?" One modern songwriter described the love of God in terms that ignited a small controversy on social media. Using the phrase "Reckless Love," worship leader Cory Asbury found himself in a conundrum. Some felt that the term "reckless"was not an appropriate way to describe God's love.

Our complaints about radical depictions of God's love often reveal more about *us* than they do about *God*. We have such a tendency to discount the love of God. In my view, the more entrenched we are in our own self-righteousness, the less sensitive we will be to the overwhelming love of God.

One story in the Gospels involved Jesus and an interchange with a sinful woman. This woman was most likely a prostitute, and yet, she discovered something about the love of God.

> *One of the Pharisees asked him to eat with him... and behold, a woman of the city, who was a sinner, when she learned that he was reclining at table in the Pharisee's house, brought an alabaster flask of ointment, and standing behind him at his feet, weeping, she began to wet his feet with her tears and wiped them with the hair of her head and kissed his feet and anointed them with the ointment. Now when the Pharisee who had invited him saw this, he said to himself, "If this man were a prophet, he would have known who and what sort of woman this is who is touching him, for she is a sinner."*
> **Luke 7:36-39**

This is a story that creates questions. Why would Jesus choose to allow this interaction in the home of a religious leader? What was it about Jesus that drew this woman? The Pharisee himself has questions. Can the holy be defiled by the unholy? Who is this man that allows such chaos around him?

Jesus responds with a story:

> *"A certain moneylender had two debtors. One owed five hundred denarii, and the other fifty. When they could not pay, he cancelled the debt of both. Now which of them will love him more?" Simon answered, "The one, I suppose, for whom he cancelled the larger debt." And he said to him, "You have judged rightly... Therefore I tell you, her sins, which are many, are forgiven—for she loved much. But he who is forgiven little, loves little." And he said to her, "Your sins are forgiven." Then those who were at table with him began to say among themselves, "Who is this, who even forgives sins?" And he said to the woman, "Your faith has saved you; go in peace."*
> **Luke 7:40-50**

Place yourself in the story...where do you fit? Do you feel more like the Pharisee... judgmental and slightly confused about God's love? Or do you identify with the sinful woman, desperate to show gratitude to Jesus?

Understanding the depth of what Jesus has done for us will sensitize us to the power of God's love. This is part of your identity. You are a much forgiven person, loved with a great love.

⚍ 26 ⚍

WE ARE
SPIRITUALLY
ALIVE

"But God, being rich in mercy, because of the great love with which he loved us, even when we were dead in our trespasses,_ made us alive together with Christ_..."
Ephesians 2:4-5

We are spiritually alive with Christ and the life of God in us is meant to transform and touch us completely - the whole way through. Our minds, bodies, and spirits are all renewed in Christ as we continue on the identity journey.

"Now may the God of peace himself sanctify you completely, and may your whole spirit and soul and body be kept blameless at the coming of our Lord Jesus Christ."
1 Thessalonians 5:23

This verse describes three parts of a human: the spirit, the soul, and the body (underlined above). God desires for the life of His Spirit to transform these three aspects of our life - spirit, soul and body.

Our manifold nature as people (spirit, soul, and body) is critical to our understanding of spiritual life. Although we are now alive in Christ, we were once dead. The life of Jesus impacts us on every possible level.

Let's define terms described in 1 Thessalonians 5 below:

+ Body: The b*ody* of a person is their physical frame, which experiences growth, entropy, and the five human senses. When you visualize a person you are thinking of his or her body.

+ Soul: The s*oul* of a person, literally translated "living being" by Bible dictionaries, describes one's personality, emotions, thoughts, decisions, and immaterial attributes. The soul is the immaterial and everlasting part of us that will exist after we die. St. Thomas Aquinas defines the soul as one's mind, will, and emotions.

+ Spirit: The *spirit* of a person is the seat of their spiritual life. Originating from Hebrew words like *"ruach"*, meaning breath and life-force, our spirits are where we experience life or death based upon our deliverance from the power of sin.

God designed humans to experience life on all three of these levels - physical life, soul life, and spiritual life. The great story of the Bible is the story of God's restoration of life. Consider this truth that we are "spiritually alive" in the context of the Bible's grand narrative.

1. **Creation - God creates life.** Upon creation, Adam and Eve were alive in every way - spirit, soul, and body. They experienced unbroken fellowship with God and communion on every level. In God's original design, called "Eden," or "Paradise," death was not present in the world.

2. **The Fall - Sin brings death.** Sadly, Adam and Eve disrupted this state of bliss through their choice to ignore God's commands. Adam and Eve sinned and disobeyed God (Bible teachers commonly refer to this event as *The Fall)*. Here, sin entered the picture and as a result, death. Sin became a fatal virus that spread to all people and the outcome was death. Death spread to all men because of their sin.

   "Therefore, just as sin came into the world through one man, and death through sin, and so death spread to all men because all sinned..."
   Romans 5:12

Today, when a person is born, they do not experience life on every level. We are born physically alive, with a soul… but *do not naturally experience spiritual life*. As a result of of sin our default position is spiritual separation from God.

3. **Redemption - New life through Jesus.** If this is the state of a man after the arrival of sin, how does someone experience God's life? How are we freed from the weight of sin and death? In Jesus's words, we must be *born again*.

   "Truly, truly, I say to you, unless one is born again he cannot see the kingdom of God." Nicodemus said to him, "How can a man be born when he is old? Can he enter a second time into his mother's womb and be born?" Jesus answered, "Truly, truly, I say to you, unless one is born of water and the Spirit, he cannot enter the kingdom of God. That which is born of the flesh is flesh, and that which is born of the Spirit is spirit."
   John 3:3-6

   Jesus explains that He is not speaking of a physical birth (being physically born in one's old age). He is speaking of a spiritual birth bringing spiritual life.

   When we begin to walk with God, we breathe in God's abundant life. Life enters into our heart from the Holy Spirit on every level - spirit, soul and body.

   How good is this life that Jesus promises? He does not simply give life to our bodies but He also will heal our bodies. He does not simply give life to our souls but He also restores our souls. And He does not simply give us spiritual life but He provides us deep spiritual fellowship with Him. Our redemption is a re-birth, a new life.

4. **Restoration - Heaven is eternal life.** At the end of the age there will be no more death (Revelation 21:4). Life on every level will be restored for all eternity. How glorious!

God loves life! Our salvation is not merely a spiritual transaction - it is an invitation to a new way of living in a new identity.

After all, as Irenaeus said, "the glory of God is man fully alive."

THE GLORY
OF GOD
IS MAN
FULLY ALIVE.

WE ARE
SEATED IN
HEAVENLY PLACES

*"…and raised us up with him and <u>seated us with him in the heavenly places</u>
in Christ Jesus."*
Ephesians 2:6

What does it mean to be seated in heavenly places with Christ Jesus? Personally this is a Scripture that I have meditated upon and struggled to apply. It seems like such a powerful idea that we are seated above our current problems and perspective with the Lord. But how does this practically take place?

God revealed more clarity to me in an unexpected way.

The answer came while watching "The Last Jedi," a recent Star Wars film, with a friend. The "The Last Jedi" is an epic final confrontation between the "dark side" and the "light side" of "the Force," a mystical balance in the universe between good and evil. In the battle, Luke Skywalker confronts Kylo Ren, his former protege' who has fallen to the dark side. During their grand Jedi battle, Kylo Ren finds Skywalker impenetrable and unbeatable, even though Ren's dark powers make him the stronger opponent.

[Spoiler Alert!]

As Ren reaches out to destroy Skywalker, Skywalker vanishes in front of him. We see that through the power of the Force that Luke had actually *bi-located*, that is, been in two places at one time, for this important battle.

We find that Luke is sitting on an island, peacefully meditating as he gains victory in the battle. Luke was in fact, not in the battle at all, but somehow in two places at once by using his Jedi meditation powers. Cool!

It was during this big reveal that my friend James turned around and said "Dude! Seated in Heavenly Places!"

As I thought about this interaction I began to wonder if it reflected a greater spiritual reality. Could it be that our meditation on who we are in Christ gives us an authority beyond what we naturally possess?

Now before you laugh at me for finding spiritual meaning in a Star Wars movie, consider this:

✤ **Because we are seated in Heavenly Places, we are <u>protected.</u>**

   Jedi Luke was impenetrable to the enemy not because of his physical strength but because of his true position. It is true that the evil one can attack and influence our day to day life but our ultimate victory is in Christ. Eternally speaking we are impenetrable.

✤ **Because we are seated in Heavenly Places, we are <u>powerful</u>.**

   Jesus taught us to pray "On earth as it is in Heaven." God has put the potential of bringing Heaven to earth in every believer. This includes miraculous exploits like the healing of the sick and also the power to transform culture. Our seat in Heavenly Places allows us to bring God's presence to every situation.

✤ **Because we are seated in Heavenly Places, we are <u>peaceful</u>.**

   Perspective always makes our problems look smaller. Our day to day struggles and administrative frustrations seem much less significant in the light of God's power and presence. We are seated above.

Although the phrase itself is a great cosmic mystery, to some extent we are in a similar position to Luke Skywalker. We are seated in a different realm with protection, power, and peace above the attack of our Enemy. I pray that you receive Heaven's perspective on your problems today. You are seated in Heavenly Places.

≈ 28 ≈

WE HAVE
RECEIVED A FREE GIFT
FROM GOD

"For by grace you have been saved through faith. And this is not your own doing; it is the gift of God, not a result of works, so that no one may boast."
Ephesians 2:8-9

"Game changer" is a relatively new term, having only been introduced into English dictionaries in 1993. The phrase means "*a newly introduced element or factor that changes an existing situation or activity in a significant way.*"

I have found in my own life and in the lives of others that a revelation of God's grace can be significant game changer in one's spiritual life. Paul mysteriously writes in 1 Corinthians about an "experience of grace." What could this mean?

"I wanted to come to you first, so that you might have a second experience of grace."
2 Corinthians 1:15

Although Bible commentators debate the exact meaning of Paul's terms I have found this saying to be true: many Christians need a "second experience of grace."

Grace is very contrary to the way our world operates. Our world operates according to the power of wealth, physical strength, and social status. Grace is given by divine favor., so we could not "boast" in our own strength. (Ephesians 2:8). Because of grace, God gets glory.

How do you know if you need a deeper understanding of God's grace?

If we rely on our own strength too long , we will reach the end of our efforts. God will use pruning, discipline, or circumstances to get our attention. We cannot finish with our own strength what God began by His Spirit. "For only crazy people would think they could complete by their own efforts what was begun by God" (Galatians 3:3, MSG). God is very intent on His will being accomplished by His strength, not ours.

In the middle of burn out, brokenness, or the "dark night of the soul,"as some Christian authors may refer to it, we will find again our need for grace. If you have found yourself in religious routine or burn out, God desires for you to have a "second experience of grace," a *grace awakening*.

Our self-strength is nothing when compared to what is available to us when living by God's grace and favor! When we surrender to God's grace, His truth brings fruitfulness. God is able to supernaturally support our work when we are willing to rely on Him. Our reaping begins to far exceed our sowing.

> *"But by the grace of God I am what I am, and his grace toward me was not in vain. On the contrary, I worked harder than any of them, though it was not I, but the grace of God that is with me."*
> **1 Corinthians 15:10**

"By the grace of God I am what I am." Your identity in Christ has been give to you by grace. And, God's grace empowers you today to accomplish His purposes. Refuse to live by self-strength. Watch what God is doing in your life and respond to Him.

The gift of grace is the ultimate game changer. Grace is not only the free gift of salvation given to the lost, it is also the supernatural empowerment of God to accomplish the will of God.

Make a fresh choice today to live by faith in God's grace. You have received it as a free gift from God.

⸗ 29 ⸗

WE HAVE MORE GRACE AND KINDNESS THAN CAN BE MEASURED

> *"…so that in the coming ages he might show the immeasurable <u>riches of his grace and kindness</u> toward us in Christ Jesus."*
> **Ephesians 2:7**

The year 2017 marked the 500th anniversary of the "Reformation," which took place in Europe during the 1500's. During this season the new technology of the printing press empowered Christians to read the Scriptures in their native tongues for the first time. Once immersed in the Scriptures, the church as a whole renewed and rediscovered the doctrines of God's *grace*.

Theologians like Martin Luther, famous for his *95 Theses*, went from town to town proclaiming the grace of God and the reality that we are saved by faith, through grace.

> *"The true treasure of the church is the most holy gospel of the glory and grace of God."*
> **Martin Luther**

In today's passage, Paul writes that God's grace will be further revealed in the "coming ages." The term can mean a "period of time," "eternity," or a "season." The Reformation of 500 years ago is a period of time that represented one such "age."

We are also promised more ages to come. Amazing! The world awaits many potential "reformations" as God reveals more and more of His grace.

For whatever season we find ourselves in throughout all eternity, God will always have an additional grace, an additional gift, and an additional means of empowerment for us. His riches are immeasurable. He does not run out.

It is remarkable that He directs His grace and kindness towards *us.* There is always more! We will worship God for all eternity because His nature is immeasurable and unfathomable by human standards.

During a time of prayer in 2017 I had an experience that was almost like a vision from the Lord. It is hard to explain, but it was almost like in this prayerful vision I saw outer space. I could see stars, planets, nebulas, galaxies, and black holes. In this time of prayer, I envisioned something similar to the end of the observable universe. As I saw stars and other heavenly objects pass through my imagination, all of a sudden everything became black.

I had a sense of God's presence and divine order even in the darkest unexplored parts of the galaxy. I felt a deep sense of peace and acceptance. This Scripture somewhat describes the awe I felt in my soul.

> *"Where shall I go from your Spirit? Or where shall I flee from your presence? If I ascend to heaven, you are there! If I make my bed in Sheol, you are there!"*
> **Psalm 139:7-8**

At the end of this time of prayer, God spoke to my heart, saying, "At the end of everything… is grace."

The current measurable universe is 93,000,000,000 light years. If we have more grace and kindness towards us in Christ Jesus than can be measured, then God's intention for us is bigger even than that!

There is truly more grace available to us in Jesus Christ than can be measured, imagined, or thought upon. Don't limit God's grace to your own human understanding. Step into a place of faith in God's sovereignty today. He has more for you than can be measured.

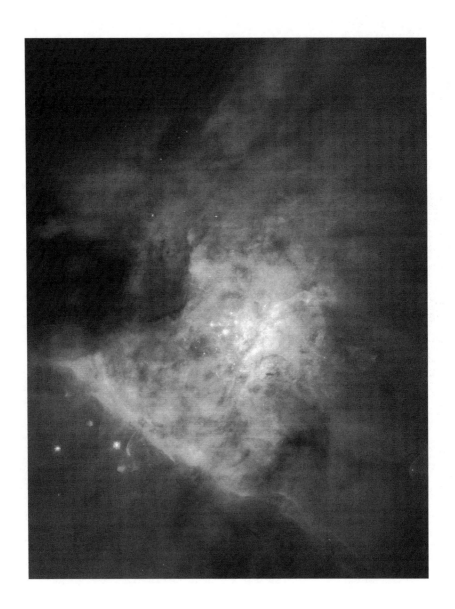

AT THE END OF EVERYTHING IS GRACE.

≈ 30 ≈

WE ARE
GOD'S
WORKMANSHIP

"For we are his <u>workmanship</u>..."
Ephesians 2:10

A *Stradivarius* is a stringed instrument, built during the 17th and 18th centuries by the Stradivari family of Italy. The instruments are known worldwide by musicians as having a unique quality of sound and craftsmanship that has been unmatched to this day. Stradivarius instruments are also collector's items, with only 650 having ever been made. The Metropolitan Museum of Art holds a collection of *Strads* on display.

A typical Stradivaius violin is worth over three million dollars. The price and musical reputation of these rare instruments has led many musicologists and economists to study their value. What makes a Stradivarius so valuable? Is its sound truly unique? Does the reputation justify the price?

Claudia Fritz, an acoustics researcher at the National Center for Scientific Research, decided to put the value of a Stradivarius to the test. Fritz gathered professional violinists in a hotel room in Indianapolis and supplied them with six violins. Amongst the violins were two Strads, another antique violin, and three modern instruments. All the participants wore dark googles and even nose plugs so that there would be no chance of their distinguishing between the instruments, with the exception being sound quality.

The researchers told the participants, *"These are all excellent violins and at least one is a Stradivarius. Play each one, and then tell us which of them is a Stradivarius."*

At the end of the study researchers found that there was no discernible difference between the Stradivarius and the more modern instruments. When the 17 players were asked to choose which is which, "Seven said they couldn't, seven got it wrong, and only three got it right."

This experiment has been repeated in Paris and New York concert halls with similar results. Researchers found that the Stradivarius had no unique value in terms of its musical quality. This of course led to a very natural question: *What then, determines the value of a Stradivarius? What makes the instruments so special and different?*

After all that study, researchers uncovered a simple truth. The value of a Stradivarius does not come from its quality of music, the songs it can play, or some special and unique tone. The value of a Stradivarius is simply derived because of who designed, made, and crafted it. The violin is valuable because of its creator and the story behind the making.

If we are "God's workmanship," then what does this say about us?

We are made by God. As people who have been fearfully and wonderfully made by God, crafted together in our mother's womb, we have immense value. A major key to understanding the power of your identity in Christ is that your value does not come out from your physical appearance, your occupation, your material success, or even your religious performance.

You are significant because God is significant, and He created you. As a result, you have immense value to God and others. Don't place your value in the music you play. Instead, be aware that your distinct value comes from your divine origin.

> *"See what great love the Father has lavished on us, that we should be called children of God! And that is what we are!"*
> **1 John 3:1**

You are God's workmanship, so your significance and self-worth comes from Him. This is the cornerstone of the identity journey.

GOD IS OUR MAKER AND OUR VALUE COMES FROM HIM.

≈ 31 ≈

WE ARE
CREATED
TO DO GOOD WORKS

"For we are his workmanship, <u>created in Christ Jesus for good works,</u> which God prepared beforehand, that we should walk in them."
Ephesians 2:10

A popular phrase goes like this, "we are human beings, not human doings." I appreciate the sentiment and yet, God did create us to *do something*. We are created to do "good works".

We live in such a tension between identity and performance. Since Adam and Eve ate of the tree of the knowledge of good and evil, humans have been empowered to categorize. We categorize experiences, sins, morality, and yes, people. We separate ourselves from others by determining rank and file... and the easiest way to make these determinations is by measuring our activity - our income, our education, our attractiveness, and our influence. Our tendency is to find our identity out of what we do rather than who God says we are.

The largest portion of this book has been devoted to you determining that your identity in Christ is determined by *eternals* and not *externals*. In God's eyes, your identity is not determined by what you do... but by what Jesus did for you. We are God's workmanship, like the beautiful Stradivarius, our value is derived from our maker, not from the music we play... and that's enough.

However, identity and function are two very different things. A Stradivarius still has a function - to play music. Think of the tragedy of owning a priceless violin that was never played, a prize horse that was never galloped, or an exotic car that was never driven. These things were created for a reason, to do something, as were we.

The Bible states that we were created for a purpose, *"to do good works."*

This assignment to do good works is part of being made in the image of God. God made it plain from the beginning of Creation. He is a "maker," a worker, (Genesis 1:1) and we were made in His image, to do good works like Him.

> *"Then God said, "Let us <u>make</u> human beings in our image, to be like us. They will <u>reign</u> over the fish in the sea, the birds in the sky, the livestock, all the wild animals on the earth, and the small animals that scurry along the ground.*
>
> *So God <u>created</u> human beings in his own image. In the image of God he <u>created</u> them; male and female he <u>created</u> them.*
>
> *Then God blessed them and said, "Be fruitful and <u>multiply</u>. <u>Fill</u> the earth and <u>govern</u> it. <u>Reign</u> over the fish in the sea, the birds in the sky, and all the animals that scurry along the ground."*
> **Genesis 1:26-28, NLT**

Note the underlined words above. Think of the activity, the blessing, the power that God gave to His ultimate creation, people. The Bible uses words like "create," "reign," "fill,"and "govern." These are words of great passion and action. This is what we were created for, to do good works in His image.

Think of the word's of Jesus's Great Commission, His last words, commanded His disciples to "go" (Matthew 28:19). In eternity, the Bible says, God's saints will "reign on the earth" (Revelation 5:10).

> *"For if, because of one man's trespass, death reigned through that one man, much more will those who receive the abundance of grace and the free gift of righteousness reign in life through the one man Jesus Christ."*
> **Romans 5:17, ESV**

What does it look like to step into the good purposes, the good works. that God intends us to do?

As we mature in Christ, God upgrades our spiritual operating system. Spiritual growth happens in stages and the Lord is very intent on our productive maturity.

We will always be God's beloved sons and daughters - but God's desire is for us to build upon that foundation. He wants to raise us up as warriors, lovers, kings and queens and ultimately, mentors to the next generation. We are destined to reign, fill the earth, and subdue it for the glory of God.

My prayer for you as you finish this 31 day devotional is that your foundation and security is so established in God's acceptance, love and plans for you that the Holy Spirit is able to build upon that foundation. I am praying for your maturity and that the Lord would begin to mold you into the kind of person who can "reign on the earth."

As I am reminded of my schooling I am always aware that promotion requires a test. In order to advance to the grade ahead a student typically must complete some kind of standardized test to prove his or her mastery of the knowledge of the previous grade. Our promotion into kings and queens will require tests, too. God allows trials and tests for our promotion. He has more good works for us to do, as we are made in His image.

> *"He will push us over the edge of the cliff... He has made us eagles like Himself. He is a mighty master eagle. He has given us His Nature. He has given us His ability. And He will not be happy until we reproduce it in our own lives."*
> **Ern Baxter**

Don't be afraid. "Be strong and courageous." God has created you to do good works. As your identity in Him begins to solidify and mature you will find what He intends you to do. He will bring the work He began to completion.

> *"And I am sure of this, that he who began a good work in you will bring it to completion at the day of Jesus Christ."*
> **Philippians 1:6**

═ Epilogue ═

IDENTITY AND
INHERITANCE

At the beginning of this devotional I wrote about a powerful experience I had concerning 31 promises from God in the book of Ephesians. The fruit of that encounter is what you have been reading for the last 31 chapters.

During that encounter with God I had another very specific promise from the Lord. I felt impressed to write in my journal a list of 31 nations in the earth. Some of them I had visited but others I have not. At the end of that time I felt the Lord speak to me, saying, "You will have influence in these 31 nations." It was an experience much like what I believe David was writing about in Psalm 2 when He overhead a cosmic conversation…

> *"Ask of me, and I will make the nations your heritage, and the ends of the earth your possession."*
> **Psalm 2:8**

Our identity has an inheritance attached to it. As we become established in our identity in Christ, God will give us specific promises and assignments for our life. How those promises get fulfilled, however, can sometimes be a mystery. We must trust God's seasons of promise and fulfillment.

Shortly after that encounter with God my family was preparing for some home renovations and I lost the journal containing that list of 31 nations. I have thought about the journal often over the last 4 years, always with a twinge of frustration towards myself for being disorganized.

This all came to a head one night after I was driving home from a church event.

I had just finished overseeing the production and logistics for a missions conference that hosted over 1,500 people. The conference was a powerful time, with many young people surrendering their lives to God's call. On the way home from that event though I felt a dissatisfaction growing in my soul. I imagine it's a little how Solomon felt when he began to consider his success a "vanity."

Although I was so grateful for the lives touched and transformed at that conference, I felt personally empty. I began to cry out to God in the car. "God, I love leading conferences… but I also desire something more for my life than simply leading church meetings. I want to be on mission with you in the world." It was a tired, vulnerable prayer at the end of a long weekend.

Later that night Shelly and I were preparing for a mentor and friend of mine to stay in our guest flat below our home. I was astonished that, after years of looking, I found that journal on a shelf in our guest room. I'd probably passed by it one hundred times. The feeling of God speaking began to return to me as I turned through that Moleskine, finding the pages where I felt God had laid 31 nations on my heart. It was so encouraging.

Later that night, about 11PM, I had to pick up our guest from the train station in downtown San Diego. It was late, so I was trying to stay awake during the drive back home. I told Joe, a spiritual father of mine, the story of the journal. Hoping for some encouragement, I said the words *"I think it was a sign!"*

Interestingly enough, after I said those words, I looked up. We were passing by a gas station. On the awning were printed the words *"THIS IS A SIGN."*

I love God's signs! My hope for you is after you become firmly established in your identity in Christ that God would begin to release signs, evidence and indications of His future plans for your life. For some people, like me, it may be hidden promises in an old journal that the Lord brings back to the forefront of your life. For others it may be an entirely new assignment. Regardless of what God has for your future I know that the best is yet to come! May you be blessed to discover your spiritual inheritance as you continue the identity journey.

> *"He has shown his people the power of his works, in giving them the inheritance of the nations."*
> **Psalm 111:6**

≈ Notes ≈

REFERENCES

GENERAL REFERENCES
- ✤ Anderson, Neil. "Victory Over the Darkness." Regal Books. 2013.
- ✤ Merriam-Webster's Collegiate Dictionary (10th ed.). (1999). Springfield, MA: Merriam-Webster Incorporated
- ✤ Strong, James. Strong's Expanded Exhaustive Concordance of the Bible. Nashville: Thomas Nelson, 2009.

COVER ART
- ✤ Photograph by Daniel Månsson, used with permission.

INTRODUCTION
- ✤ The Apostle's Creed is a historic creed of the Christian church. I have included the "ecumenical version" of the creed in the preface of this book.
- ✤ Quotation from "Gospel in Life Study Guide" by Tim Keller,: Zondervan, 2010.

DAY 1
- ✤ Photograph courtesy of unsplash.com.

DAY 2
- ✤ I first learned of the "first five minute rule" through the writings of Dr. James Dobson.

DAY 3
- ✤ Photograph of WR Grace building courtesy of Garrett Rowland, used with permission.

DAY 6
- ✤ Taken from the "The Westminster Confession of Faith". 3rd ed. Lawrenceville, GA: Committee for Christian Education and Publications, 1990.

DAY 9
- ✤ Quotation from "Bono: In Conversation with Michka Assayas." by Michka Assayas, copyright © 2005 by Michka Awwayas. Riverhead Books, an imprint of Penguin Group (USA) Inc.

DAY 10
- ✤ Quotation from "Warren, Rick. The Purpose Driven Life. Michigan: Zondervan, 2002. "
- ✤ Photograph by Matthew Clark Rogers, used with permission.

DAY 12
- ✤ Groth, Aimee. "Entrepreneurs don't have a special gene for risk…" Quartz. July 17, 2015.

DAY 14
- ✤ Photograph of Princeton seal courtesy of wikipedia.org.

DAY 15
- ✤ Raspberry, William. "Poverty and the Father Factor." Washington Post. Monday August 1, 2005.

DAY 16
- ✤ Booker, Christopher. "The Seven Basic Plots." Bloomsbury. 2004.

DAY 19
- ✤ Frankl, Victor. "Man's Search for Meaning." Beacon Press. 1959.

DAY 20
- ✤ Photograph of Trinity Church, New York courtesy of wikipedia.org.

DAY 21
- ✤ The book I refer to is "The Fire of the North" by David Adam.
- ✤ Quotation from "Benedict. The Vatican. Accessed online 12/6/18. http://w2.vatican.va."

- For more information on the impact and spiritual history of the Celtic Church I suggest reading "How the Irish Saved Civilization" by Thomas Cahill.
- Photograph courtesy of Daniel Månsson, used with permission.

DAY 22
- I learned about this story of Robert Cumming's experience with "The Virgin and Child..." through Nicky Gumbel's Bible in One Year (bibleinoneyear.org)
- Artistic reproduction of Filipino Lippi's "The Virgin and Child with Saints Jerome and Dominic" courtesy of The London National Gallery Online.

DAY 23
- Photograph courtesy of The London National Gallery Online.

DAY 24
- Mark Whitaker, "Billy Graham Messenger of Hope." Two Ten Magazine. 4th Quarter, 2013.

DAY 26
- Aquinas, Thomas. "Summa Theologica." 1274.
- Photograph by Daniel Månsson, used with permission.

DAY 29
- Quotation taken from Thesis 62 of Martin Luther's 95 Theses.
- Photograph courtesy of NASA Online.

DAY 30
- I learned about the Stradivarius study from the NPR "Planet Money" Podcast, Episode 538, Published June 22, 2106.
- Artistic reproduction of Edgar Degas's "Violinist, Study for Dance Lesson" courtesy of the Metropolitan Museum of Art Online.

DAY 31
- Quotation from the remarkable sermon "Life on Wings" by Ern Baxter.

AUTHOR PHOTOGRAPH
- Photograph by Katie Scott, used with permission.

Notes

SPECIAL THANKS

Thanks to my wife Shelly for her support in this project. Proverbs 18:22.

This book would not have been possible without the investment and encouragement of my friend, Daniel Månsson.

I would also like to extend a very special thank you to my editing team, Emily McLenachen, Derralyn Short, Hannah Weatherred, Tiffany Valdez.

Thank you Sara Combs for providing your input on the design.

⚡ About the Author ⚡

KENDALL LAUGHLIN, JR.

Kendall Laughlin, Jr. resides in the San Diego area where he serves on the leadership of All Peoples Church. His desire is to equip others to reign in life. To learn more about Kendall and find more resources by him, visit his website, *KALJR.COM*.

Made in the USA
San Bernardino, CA
20 January 2019